Become a Business Analyst:

Real Life CASE STUDIES with solutions to help you LEARN FAST and CRACK INTERVIEWS!

By Manmeet Singh

Table of Contents

3

Prologue

In an era where the fusion of technology, strategy, and data-driven insights fuels business success, the role of a Business Analyst has evolved into an indispensable asset. Whether you are an aspiring Business Analyst, a seasoned professional seeking growth, or simply intrigued by the multifaceted world of business analysis, this comprehensive guide is your key to unlocking this thriving profession.

"Become a Business Analyst: Real Life CASE STUDIES with solutions to help you LEARN FAST and CRACK INTERVIEWS!" transcends the conventional approaches, offering you a hands-on exploration of business analysis. From understanding the ubiquity of business analysis and assessing your inherent aptitude, to exploring Agile and Waterfall methodologies, this book spans the gamut of knowledge required to thrive as a Business Analyst.

With a rich collection of case studies covering diverse scenarios such as Ecommerce Store Enhancements, AI-Enhanced Operational Efficiency, and Inclusive Labor Market Strategies, you'll embark on an insightful journey. Each case study, meticulously crafted, introduces you to unique business challenges, strategies, and solutions. You'll delve into writing Epics and User Stories, analyzing solution options, and much more.

But this book is not just about theories and methodologies. It's a practical roadmap for career progression, packed with real-life interviews, resume preparation tips, and valuable job search insights. It's about nurturing your analytical acumen, sharpening your problem-solving prowess, and gearing you up for successful interviews.

The chapters within these pages go beyond giving you the tools to think, solve, and become a Business Analyst. They inspire, guide, and instil the confidence required to navigate the ever-changing landscape of business analysis. Whether you are driven by curiosity, career aspirations, or a blend of both, this book promises a rewarding and empowering experience.

Welcome to "Become a Business Analyst." Join me as we delve into real case studies, unfold critical insights, and pave our path to success together. Your exciting journey into the realm of business analysis awaits.

Your Game Plan: Maximizing the Value from This Book

Congratulations on taking the first step towards unlocking a rewarding career as a Business Analyst. To make the most of this book, here's a suggested game plan:

1. Build Your Foundation: Start by understanding the basics of business analysis. The chapters "The Ubiquity of Business Analysis" and "Business Analysis in a Corporate Landscape" will provide you with a solid foundation on the role, responsibilities, and the context in which a business analyst operates.

2. Learn the Concepts: Delve into the seven case studies featured in this book. Each case study highlights a unique business problem and its solution, providing you an opportunity to learn and apply key business analysis concepts in real-world scenarios.

3. Apply Your Knowledge: After understanding the theory, it's time to put your knowledge into action. Use the "Business Analyst Resume Preparation" chapter to craft a compelling resume that highlights your newly gained knowledge and skills.

4. Prepare for the Interview: Go through the chapter "Business Analyst Job Interview" to familiarize yourself with common interview questions and successful strategies for answering them. The real-life interview responses from a seasoned Senior Business Analyst and an ambitious Graduate Business Analyst will provide you with practical insights.

5. Leverage Certifications: The chapter "Free Business Analyst Certifications for your resume" will guide you on how to further enhance your professional credibility through relevant certifications.

6. Job Hunting: Finally, use the "Business Analyst Job Search Tips" chapter to kickstart your job search and learn how to identify suitable opportunities effectively.

Remember, the journey towards becoming a Business Analyst is not a sprint but a marathon. Take the time to read, understand, and apply the concepts outlined in this book. Patience, persistence, and the right approach will set you on the path to a successful career in business analysis.

Good luck on your journey!

Action-Based Money Back Guarantee

We stand behind the value that 'Become a Business Analyst: Real Life CASE STUDIES with solutions to help you LEARN FAST and CRACK INTERVIEWS!' provides. However, if after reading the book, applying the strategies, and implementing the following actions you do not see a noticeable improvement in your business analysis skills or job prospects within 30 days, we will provide a full refund of your purchase price.

The actions are as follows:

1. Complete reading the book.

2. Prepare a Business Analyst resume, using the guidelines provided in the book.

3. Apply to at least 3 job openings, using the job search strategies recommended in the book.

To request a refund, contact us via email at BACareerStrategy@gmail.com within 30 days of your purchase. Please include proof that you completed all the action-based steps with your request for a refund along with proof of purchase and feedback constructive feedback on why the book did not meet your expectations.

We believe in the power of action and learning, and if you've genuinely given your best effort and not seen results, we believe it's fair to return your investment.

The Ubiquity of Business Analysis

The concept of business analysis might seem abstract and confined to corporate meeting rooms but Business Analysis isn't just about improving business processes or implementing new IT systems; at its core, it's about problem-solving and decision-making. These are skills we all use regularly, even if we're not professional business analysts.

For example, have you ever planned a family holiday or renovated your home? Maybe you've had to find a tutor for your child? In all of these situations, you've had to clearly identify your needs, gather and analyze different kinds of information, evaluate various options, and make decisions based on your findings.

Does that process sound familiar? It should, because it's the core process of business analysis.

The following sections of this chapter will explore a few everyday scenarios, detailing how each stage mirrors the tasks of a business analyst. By the end of this chapter, you will not only appreciate how pervasive business analysis is but also how understanding these skills in a familiar context can demystify the role and practice of business analysis.

Now, let's look at some of these scenarios in detail...

Scenario 1: Planning a Holiday

Imagine you're planning a family vacation. You have a certain budget, you need to choose a destination, plan accommodation, decide the best time to go, what to do once you're there, and how to get there. This requires business analysis skills, as you're identifying needs (a fun, relaxing holiday within a certain budget), assessing various options, and making data-driven decisions.

First, you need to **gather requirements**. What are your family's preferences? Do they prefer a beach holiday, a city break, or an adventure trip? What activities are non-negotiable, and what can be flexible?

Then comes **research and analysis**. Comparing flight prices, hotel rates, weather trends, and user reviews, you sift through a large amount of data to find the optimal solution.

Lastly, you make your **decision**. This decision should be based on a comprehensive analysis of all your findings, including prices, reviews, and the likelihood of meeting your family's needs and wants.

This process mirrors the activities of a business analyst, who identifies business needs, analyzes data, and recommends solutions.

Scenario 2: Renovating Your Home

Next, consider you're planning to renovate your home. You need to decide what to renovate, how to do it, who should do the work, and how much you're willing to spend. Once again, your business analysis skills come into play.

Identifying needs is the first step. Do you need a larger kitchen, a second bathroom, or a new roof? What is your budget? What are your time constraints? This is similar to defining the scope of a project in business analysis.

Vendor analysis is your next step. You'll need to gather quotes from different contractors, check their references, assess their work quality, and consider their availability. It's akin to evaluating different business solutions and vendors in a corporate setting.

Risk analysis is another crucial business analysis skill. What if the renovation goes over budget? What if it isn't completed on time? Just as a business analyst would, you need to identify potential risks and develop contingency plans.

Scenario 3: Selecting a Tutor

Lastly, imagine you're selecting a tutor for your child. You need to identify the needs, find potential tutors, compare them, and make a decision.

First, **determine the needs**. What are your child's strengths and weaknesses? How much can you afford to pay? How often does your child need tutoring? The answers to these questions help define your requirements.

Comparing potential solutions is your next task. You'll need to compare the qualifications, experience, teaching methods, availability, and fees of various tutors. It's much like comparing business solutions to find the one that best meets the organization's needs.

Decision making is your final step. You'll use the information you've gathered to make a decision, just as a business analyst would after thorough research and analysis.

Cultivating Your Inner Business Analyst: Skills and Aptitude Assessment

Having delved into the ubiquitous nature of business analysis, we now turn our attention to the key skills that a business analyst should possess and how one can determine if a career in business analysis might be the right path.

Key Skills for a Business Analyst

1. **Problem-Solving:** This is at the heart of business analysis. An effective business analyst can identify problems, analyze them, and propose solutions that meet business objectives.

2. **Communication:** Business analysts need to be effective communicators, able to listen, articulate ideas, and facilitate conversations between different stakeholders.

3. **Analytical Thinking:** Business analysts must have the ability to gather, analyze, and interpret data to drive decision-making processes.

4. **Detail-Oriented:** Precision and attention to detail are crucial for creating accurate reports, specifications, and project plans.

5. **Negotiation and Persuasion:** Business analysts often need to negotiate with stakeholders and persuade them to accept certain solutions or changes.

6. **Project Management:** Business analysts should have a good understanding of project management principles

and methodologies, whether Agile or Waterfall, to ensure project goals are met.

7. **Technical Proficiency:** While not always necessary, understanding technologies related to the business can be a valuable asset. This might involve knowledge of software development, databases, systems architecture, and more.

Self-Assessment: Is Business Analysis Right for You?

Reflect on the following questions to assess whether business analysis could be a potential career path:

1. **Do you enjoy solving problems?** As mentioned earlier, problem-solving is at the core of business analysis. If you derive satisfaction from dissecting complex situations and finding solutions, business analysis could be a good fit for you.

2. **Are you comfortable with ambiguity?** In the initial stages of a project, many things may not be clear. You must be comfortable navigating through ambiguity and uncertainty to define clear requirements and strategies.

3. **Do you enjoy working with others?** Business analysts often work as a bridge between various stakeholders. This involves working closely with different people, understanding their perspectives, and managing their expectations.

4. **Are you a good communicator?** Effective communication is vital in this role. You should be comfortable

communicating complex information to diverse audiences.

5. **Do you have a keen eye for detail?** Business analysts need to pay attention to small details while keeping an eye on the big picture.

6. **Are you a quick learner?** Business analysts often work across various domains and technologies. The ability to learn quickly and adapt to new environments is a valuable asset.

7. **Do you have a knack for persuasion?** Sometimes, a business analyst may need to convince stakeholders to adopt a particular solution or change.

If you find yourself answering 'yes' to most of these questions, you might be well-suited for a career in business analysis. This journey, while challenging, can be extremely rewarding, offering opportunities to drive impactful changes within an organization.

Business Analysis in a corporate landscape

Building on the ubiquity of business analysis, we delve into its role within the corporate world, where these skills are often formalized and magnified. Whether within a startup or a multinational corporation, businesses operate with projects - distinct, purposeful initiatives that bring about specific, often transformative, changes. Let's delve into real-world examples, revealing how business analysis is applied in various sectors and in both IT and non-IT contexts.

1. **Banking Sector (IT Project) - Implementing a New Core Banking System:** In an effort to improve operational efficiency and customer service, a bank initiated a project to replace its aging core banking system. The business analyst played a pivotal role, liaising closely with stakeholders from various departments (like finance, operations, and customer service) to understand their needs and document the requirements. They also bridged the communication gap between the IT team and the banking software vendor to ensure the new system met all the requirements and was smoothly implemented.

2. **Retail (Non-IT Project) - Launching a New Store:** For a leading retail chain planning to open a new store in a prime location, the business analyst was involved from the very inception. They conducted market analysis, gauged the local demographics, and recommended the product mix based on these findings. Furthermore, they collaborated with the operations and logistics teams to design the store layout for optimal footfall and effective inventory management.

3. **Healthcare Sector (IT Project) - Implementing an Electronic Health Record (EHR) System:** When a large hospital decided to digitize its health records for better patient care and streamlined operations, the business analyst worked alongside doctors, nurses, administrators, and IT staff. They documented the functional and non-functional requirements for the EHR system, carried out vendor analysis, supervised user acceptance testing, and trained the staff on using the new system.

4. **Manufacturing (Non-IT Project) - Lean Manufacturing Initiative:** A manufacturing company set forth to reduce waste and enhance efficiency using lean principles. The business analyst collaborated with the operations team to map the current manufacturing processes, identify areas of waste, and recommend changes based on lean principles. They also developed key metrics to measure the success of the initiative and monitored the impact post-implementation.

5. **Public Sector (IT Project) - Digitizing Public Services:** A local government aiming to improve public services embarked on creating a digital platform for citizens to access various services like bill payments, license renewals, and reporting issues. The business analyst facilitated communication among multiple stakeholders, including citizens, public service providers, and IT developers. They translated needs into technical requirements and participated in user interface design, testing, and the platform's rollout.

These examples illustrate the broad scope of business analysis, encompassing both IT and non-IT projects across various sectors. They highlight the pivotal role a business analyst plays in bridging the gap between different stakeholders and ensuring the project meets its objectives. In the end, the business analyst serves as the anchor, keeping the project grounded to its original goals while navigating the winds of change.

Agile and Waterfall: Two Methodologies, One Goal

Whether an organization adopts Agile or Waterfall methodologies, the ultimate objective remains the same: successfully completing a project that brings value to the business. Projects, by their nature, are temporary undertakings designed to produce a unique product, service, or result with a defined beginning and end. They are carried out in an environment that is both constrained and shaped by factors such as time, cost, and quality.

Project management is the practice of guiding the process and people involved in the project towards achieving the project's goal efficiently and effectively. Depending on the specific requirements of the project and the environment in which it operates, different project management methodologies may be employed. Agile and Waterfall are two such methodologies that, while differing in approach, both aim at the systematic progression of tasks towards the project's successful completion.

Each methodology (Agile/Waterfall) has its strengths, and the choice between them depends on the nature and context of the project. Interestingly, the role of a Business Analyst can vary significantly between these two methodologies. Understanding these methodologies and the role of a Business Analyst within them is crucial to navigate the complexities of modern project environments.

The Waterfall Approach

In the traditional Waterfall model, projects are carried out in a linear, sequential manner, where each stage of the project follows the preceding stage and there's little room for changes or revisions once a stage is completed.

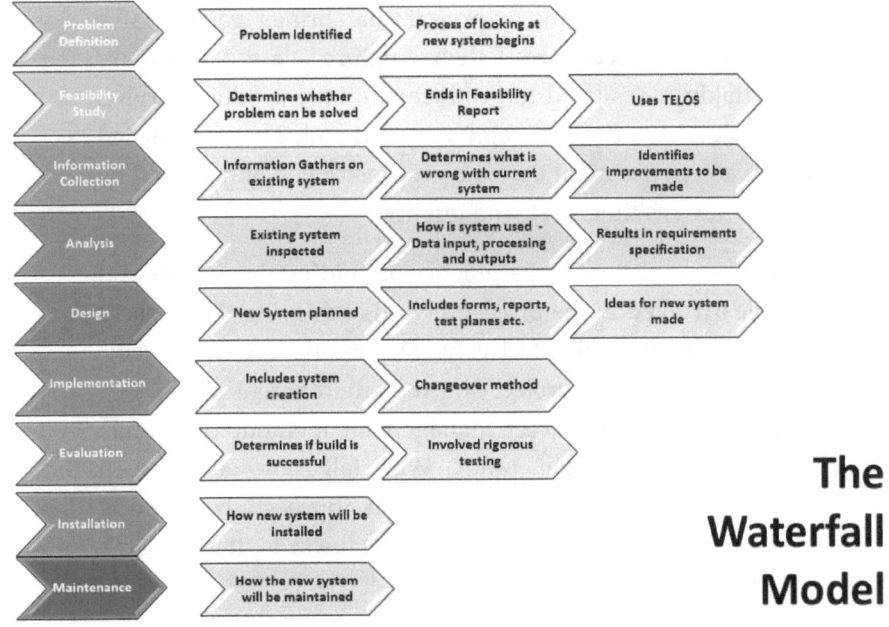

The Waterfall Model

Here, BAs often have a defined role, creating detailed project documents up-front and ensuring that all requirements are explicitly outlined before any development begins. For instance, during the "Project Planning Stage" as outlined later, BAs using the Waterfall model would likely spend significant time gathering and documenting detailed project requirements, creating extensive functional specifications and test plans.

The Agile Approach

On the other hand, Agile adopts an iterative, flexible approach. Work is divided into smaller segments known as 'sprints', and the focus is on continuous improvement in response to changes and feedback.

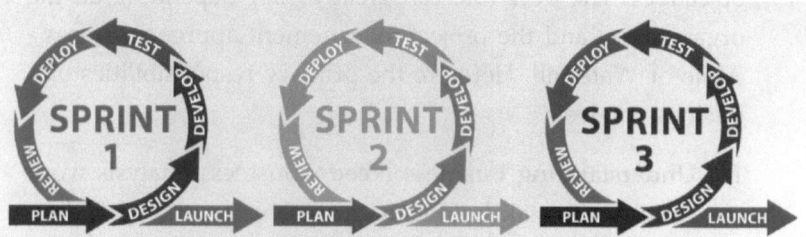

In an Agile environment, the BA's role tends to be more dynamic. Rather than focusing on extensive up-front documentation, BAs work closely with stakeholders and the development team throughout the project to iteratively refine the requirements and solutions. For example, during the "Project Execution Stage", an Agile BA might be involved in facilitating daily stand-ups, working with the Product Owner to prioritize and refine the product backlog, or collaborating with the development team to clarify requirements and accept completed work.

In both Agile and Waterfall methodologies, BAs still have the critical task of ensuring that the project aligns with business objectives. The difference lies in the way they interact with the project team and stakeholders, the level of documentation produced, and their involvement in the project lifecycle. Regardless of the methodology used, the BA's ultimate goal remains the same - to deliver value to the business.

WHAT does a Business Analyst do?

A business analyst is the vital link between an organization's IT capabilities and its business objectives, acting as a bridge between the technical team that crafts solutions and the business stakeholders who define business needs and objectives. The BA's role can greatly vary depending on the organization and the project management approach it uses - Agile or Waterfall. Here are the primary responsibilities of a business analyst:

1. **Understanding Business Needs:** Business analysts work closely with stakeholders to comprehend and define their business needs, goals, and strategies, irrespective of whether an Agile or Waterfall methodology is in use. They gather and analyze information about the business's processes, systems, and structures.

2. **Requirements Gathering:** In both Agile and Waterfall environments, business analysts are responsible for gathering, documenting, and managing business requirements for changes to business processes or systems. This often involves conducting interviews, workshops, and surveys, and then translating the findings into functional specifications and detailed test plans or user stories (in Agile).

3. **Process Modelling:** They create process models, specifications, diagrams, and charts to guide system developers and/or the project team. This could include designing new processes or improving existing ones.

4. **Solution Design and Recommendation:** Business analysts use their understanding of the business and its technology to identify solutions that meet the business's

needs, irrespective of the methodology adopted. This could involve designing a new IT solution, modifying an existing one, or even changing business processes.

5. **Project Management and Coordination:** Business analysts often play a role in coordinating or managing various stages of a project, be it an Agile sprint or a Waterfall phase. They ensure the project is in line with the business's needs, from initial planning through implementation and testing.

6. **Change Management:** In both Agile and Waterfall settings, they play a significant role in managing change within the organization. This includes helping to communicate changes, training staff, and managing any resistance to change.

7. **Data Analysis and Interpretation:** Business analysts must adeptly use data to drive decision-making, analyzing data related to business processes, market trends, or customer behavior, for example, and then use this analysis to inform their recommendations.

8. **Quality Assurance and Testing:** In some cases, business analysts may also be involved in quality assurance and testing of new systems or system modifications, regardless of whether it's an Agile or Waterfall project.

In essence, a business analyst ensures that solutions align with business objectives and are implemented effectively. Their job is to decipher the business needs, translate them into actionable plans, and work with the technical teams to realize these plans, regardless of whether the project follows an Agile or Waterfall methodology.

HOW does a Business Analyst do what they do?

A business analyst utilizes a combination of tools, methodologies, soft skills, and either Agile or Waterfall project management approaches to carry out their role effectively. Here's an in-depth look at how they perform their duties:

1. **Communication:** Business analysts spend a substantial amount of time communicating with stakeholders, project teams, and end-users. Activities might involve conducting interviews, leading meetings, or presenting findings. Clear, effective communication is critical for understanding and conveying business needs, and to align everyone with the project's objectives and progress, irrespective of whether Agile or Waterfall methodology is used.

2. **Data Analysis:** Business analysts employ various data analysis tools and techniques to understand trends, issues, or opportunities. This could involve querying databases, analyzing customer or market data, or using statistical analysis tools. The insights derived from this analysis inform the business analyst's recommendations.

3. **Documentation:** In both Agile and Waterfall methodologies, business analysts generate a host of documents, from business requirements documents and functional specifications, to process maps and user manuals, or user stories and backlogs in Agile. These documents ensure that everyone comprehends the

24

business needs and the suggested solutions, and provide a record for future reference.

4. **Problem Solving:** Business analysts are at their core, problem solvers. They need to identify problems, critically consider potential solutions, and collaborate with others to implement these solutions. Techniques can vary between brainstorming, conducting root cause analysis, or using other problem-solving methodologies.

5. **Project Management:** Irrespective of the methodology (Agile or Waterfall), business analysts often apply project management methodologies to ensure projects are delivered timely and within budget. This could involve creating project plans or sprints, coordinating resources, and monitoring progress.

6. **Modelling:** Business analysts use diverse modelling tools and techniques to visualize processes, data flows, or system architectures. Techniques like Unified Modelling Language (UML), Business Process Model and Notation (BPMN), or other modelling methodologies are applied. These models help to clarify complex systems and processes, and inform the design of solutions.

7. **Change Management:** The implementation of new systems or processes often involves significant change. Business analysts may use change management techniques to manage this change, including communicating changes, training staff, and managing resistance, in both Agile and Waterfall contexts.

8. **Requirements Engineering:** A core part of the business analyst's role is gathering, analyzing, documenting, and validating business requirements. Various techniques such as user stories (in Agile), use cases, or prototyping might be employed.

9. **Stakeholder Management:** Business analysts need to work effectively with a range of stakeholders, from senior management to end-users, regardless of the project's methodology. This could involve managing expectations, resolving conflicts, and ensuring stakeholder buy-in.

Through the combination of these skills and methodologies, a business analyst ensures that business needs are clearly understood and that solutions are designed and implemented effectively to fulfill these needs, whether the project uses an Agile or a Waterfall approach.

WHAT deliverables does a Business Analyst produce?

A Business Analyst (BA) creates a wide array of deliverables depending on the phase, needs of the project, and the methodology in use. However, here are some common deliverables that a business analyst may produce:

In a Waterfall methodology:

1. **Requirements documents**: These documents detail the business requirements and functional specifications for a project. These can include user stories, use cases, process flows, data models, and other types of requirements documentation.

2. **Business cases**: Business cases are documents that outline the business objectives, benefits, costs, and risks associated with a project. The business case provides justification for why the project should be pursued and what the expected return on investment will be.

3. **Functional specifications**: Functional specifications are detailed descriptions of the features and functions that a system or product must have to meet the business requirements. These documents are used to guide the development team in building the product.

4. **Test plans**: Test plans describe how the product will be tested to ensure that it meets the business requirements and functional specifications. The test plan outlines the test scenarios, test cases, and test data that will be used to validate the product.

5. **User manuals and training materials**: User manuals and training materials are created to help end-users

understand how to use the product. These materials provide step-by-step instructions on how to use the product and can include screenshots, videos, and other visual aids.

6. **Project plans**: Project plans are used to manage the project schedule, budget, and resources. These plans outline the project milestones, tasks, dependencies, and timelines.

7. **Change requests**: Change requests are documents that outline proposed changes to the project scope, requirements, or timeline. These documents are used to track and manage changes to the project.

8. **Stakeholder analysis reports**: These reports identify and analyze the stakeholders involved in the project. They provide information on the stakeholders' interests, goals, and potential impact on the project.

In an Agile methodology:

1. **Product Backlog:** The BA works with the Product Owner to build and prioritize the product backlog. The product backlog is a list of features, enhancements, and fixes for the product, presented as user stories.

2. **User Stories:** These are short descriptions of a feature told from the perspective of the user. User stories are often accompanied by acceptance criteria that define the scope of the story.

3. **Sprint Backlog:** For each sprint, a subset of the product backlog items is chosen, forming the sprint backlog. The BA often assists in refining these items for the Development Team.

4. **Burndown Charts:** These graphical representations show the work left to do versus time in a sprint. BAs may assist the Scrum Master in maintaining these charts.
5. **Meeting Minutes and Action Items:** In Agile, meetings like daily stand-ups, sprint planning, sprint review, and retrospectives are important. The BA may help document key decisions and action items from these meetings.

While the type of deliverables in each methodology is different, they all aim to provide the necessary information to guide the project's development and execution. These deliverables should be aligned with the project's objectives and ultimately meet the needs of the business.

WHAT work is expected from a Business Analyst?

In a Waterfall methodology:

A business analyst's work changes depending on the stage of the project. Here's a breakdown of what a business analyst typically does in each stage of a project following the Waterfall methodology:

1. **Project initiation stage:** The business analyst works with stakeholders to identify the business problem, objectives, scope, and requirements. Key tasks may include conducting a feasibility study, developing a business case, identifying and analyzing stakeholders, and creating a project charter.

2. **Project planning stage:** The business analyst supports the project manager and team members in planning and designing the project. Key tasks may include developing a project plan, conducting risk assessments, creating detailed functional and technical requirements, and coordinating with stakeholders.

3. **Project execution stage:** The business analyst ensures the project is executed according to plan. Key tasks may include monitoring project progress, conducting change management activities, facilitating communication among project team members, and identifying and resolving issues.

4. **Project monitoring and control stage:** The business analyst works with the project manager to ensure the

project stays on track. Key tasks may include monitoring project performance, updating the project plan, identifying and resolving issues, and coordinating with stakeholders.

5. **Project closure stage:** The business analyst works with the project manager to ensure the project is successfully completed. Key tasks may include conducting a final project review, preparing and presenting project documentation and reports, conducting a lessons learned session, and transitioning deliverables to stakeholders.

In an Agile methodology:

The work of a business analyst differs slightly in Agile, given the iterative nature of the methodology. Their activities often extend across all iterations (sprints) and stages of the project:

1. **Product Backlog Creation and Refinement:** Business Analysts, often in the role of Product Owner or in collaboration with them, work on creating, maintaining, and refining the product backlog. This involves identifying user stories or requirements that deliver value to the business, and prioritizing them based on factors like business value, risk, and dependencies.

2. **Sprint Planning:** Business Analysts are heavily involved in sprint planning meetings where the team decides on the user stories to be delivered in the next sprint. They help explain the requirements and acceptance criteria to the team.

3. **Sprint Execution:** During the sprint, Business Analysts often serve as a point of contact for any questions or clarifications about the user stories in progress. They also collaborate with the team and stakeholders to refine and reprioritize the backlog as needed.

4. **Review and Retrospective:** At the end of each sprint, Business Analysts play a significant role in the sprint review meeting, where the team demonstrates the implemented user stories to stakeholders. They also participate in sprint retrospectives, where the team reflects on its performance during the sprint and identifies areas for improvement.

In both methodologies, the business analyst plays a critical role in ensuring the success of a project, being involved in all stages of the project lifecycle.

A Day in the Life of a Business Analyst

Being a business analyst involves a multitude of tasks that vary depending on the project, team, and the specific methodology being used. This chapter will provide a glimpse into a typical day of a business analyst in both Agile and Waterfall contexts.

Agile Context:

The day begins with a stand-up meeting, also known as the daily scrum. The business analyst, along with the rest of the Agile team, shares updates about what they worked on the previous day, what they plan to work on today, and any obstacles they're facing. This keeps everyone aligned and aware of the project's progress and challenges.

Following this, the business analyst might have a backlog refinement or grooming session. During this, they work with the product owner and the team to review the product backlog, ensure the user stories are clear and valuable, and prioritize them based on the business value.

The rest of the day may involve facilitating story estimation sessions, working with the team to understand the size and effort of upcoming user stories, and updating the product backlog with the estimates. They may also work on creating or refining acceptance criteria for user stories to ensure they're testable and clear to the development team.

A significant part of the day might be spent liaising with stakeholders, gathering requirements for future sprints, and managing any change requests. They could also work with the Quality Assurance team, helping them understand requirements and answering any questions they might have about user stories.

The day ends with a quick check-in with the team and perhaps some time spent on project documentation.

Waterfall Context:

In a Waterfall context, the day may begin with a meeting with stakeholders or the project manager to understand or clarify project requirements. These requirements could be for a new project or a phase of the ongoing project.

The rest of the day may involve creating detailed requirement documentation, process modelling, or designing use cases. The analyst may also spend time validating the requirements with stakeholders to ensure they are complete and meet business needs.

As part of a larger project plan, the analyst may need to work with other team members to provide inputs into the project plan or understand the plan's impacts on the project's business analysis activities.

Throughout the day, the business analyst might need to manage scope, identify potential risks or issues, and communicate these to the project manager or stakeholders. They could also spend time developing a business case or conducting feasibility studies for new projects.

The day ends with perhaps a status update meeting with the project manager and some time spent updating project documentation.

Regardless of the methodology, a business analyst's day is dynamic and filled with problem-solving, critical thinking, and communication. They're continually interacting with stakeholders, managing, and refining requirements, and contributing to the overall success of their projects.

Career Progression for a Business Analyst

The role of a Business Analyst (BA) is multifaceted and challenging yet rewarding. It offers vast opportunities for career growth and progression. A BA's journey typically starts as a junior or entry-level analyst but, with experience and continued learning, can lead to senior, management, or even strategic positions within an organization. The progression often involves gaining depth in business analysis itself or branching out into related areas such as project management, product management, or consulting.

Entry-Level Business Analyst: In both Agile and Waterfall environments, individuals often start their careers as entry-level or junior BAs. Their role includes assisting senior analysts in conducting research, collecting and analyzing data, and gathering requirements. This is a learning stage, where individuals acquire foundational skills and understanding of the industry and business analysis processes.

Business Analyst: As junior BAs gain experience and expertise, they progress to become fully-fledged Business Analysts. Here, the nature of the role may diverge depending on the project management methodology in place. In a Waterfall environment, BAs may find themselves focused on extensive upfront requirements gathering and documentation, while in an Agile environment, they would be heavily involved in iterative requirement discussions, grooming product backlogs, and collaborating closely with the development team and stakeholders in each sprint.

Senior Business Analyst/Lead Business Analyst: After gaining substantial experience and demonstrating proficiency, BAs can progress to become Senior or Lead BAs. In a Waterfall setting, these individuals typically handle more complex, high-stakes projects, leading requirements gathering efforts and ensuring alignment between business needs and technical solutions. In Agile contexts, a Senior BA might take on the role of a Product Owner, prioritizing the backlog, deciding on iterations, and acting as the primary liaison between the business stakeholders and the development team.

Business Analysis Manager/Consultant: From a senior role, BAs may move into managerial or consultancy positions. They might oversee a team of analysts, manage multiple projects or a portfolio, and provide strategic inputs. The adoption of Agile or Waterfall methodologies can influence the role here, as Agile environments encourage a more collaborative, cross-functional leadership style, while Waterfall environments might have more distinct hierarchies and roles.

Product Manager/Project Manager: As a career pivot, BAs might choose to leverage their acquired skills and experience to transition into product or project management roles. In Agile environments, BAs might lean towards Product Management due to their heavy involvement with product backlogs and sprint planning. In Waterfall contexts, with their extensive project lifecycle experience, transitioning into Project Management might be a natural progression.

Chief Information Officer/Chief Technology Officer: Ultimately, seasoned BAs with a strong record of accomplishments can aspire to executive roles such as CIO or CTO. They can influence the strategic direction of an organization's IT landscape. In Agile organizations, such roles would require a strong emphasis on fostering a culture of collaboration, continuous improvement, and adaptability.

A career in business analysis offers a unique blend of business and technology, and the path can be varied and flexible. However, success in this field is not just about climbing the corporate ladder. It's about continuously learning, adapting to changes, and finding ways to create value for the business. Each stage of this progression demands a deeper understanding of business operations, improved technical skills, stronger stakeholder management abilities, and enhanced leadership competencies. Therefore, continued professional development through on-the-job learning, mentoring, and formal training and certifications is crucial.

Remember, this progression is not linear or uniform for everyone. It's influenced by factors such as the size and type of the organization, industry dynamics, individual skills and aspirations, and market trends. Therefore, it's essential for each BA to chart their unique career path and progression based on their interests, strengths, and opportunities.

Learning Business Analysis concepts: a Case Study approach

The case study approach to learning, particularly in the field of business analysis, offers a unique and incredibly effective way to understand, dissect, and tackle real-world business problems. It brings theories to life and enables learners to apply principles in practical, tangible scenarios. Each case study acts as a mini-simulation of a business challenge, where you, as the analyst, work your way through complex situations, engage stakeholders, conduct research, gather requirements, and evaluate solution options.

This method of learning is more than just passive reading; it demands active engagement and critical thinking, offering a deeper understanding of the subject matter. By grappling with real issues faced by businesses, learners can quickly grasp essential concepts, strategies, and methodologies that are often difficult to understand in the abstract.

Moreover, it allows for immediate application of knowledge, making the learning process more dynamic and impactful. The solutions provided give you the opportunity to compare, contrast, and learn from expert approaches, making you well-equipped to handle similar scenarios in the real world. Thus, a case study approach to learning is not just efficient, it's an exciting, immersive way to become a proficient business analyst.

Case Study 1: Orchestrating an Office Relocation

In this case study, we delve into an intricate project – facilitating the relocation of a team from Bristol to Peterborough. This mission is a challenging exercise in strategic planning and operational coordination.

As the assigned business analyst, you will bring your critical skills in stakeholder management, requirements gathering, and process modelling to the forefront to ensure a successful transition.

This case study touches upon various fundamental concepts in business analysis such as stakeholder management, requirements elicitation and documentation, risk assessment, and project management. It showcases how these core principles apply not just to traditional IT or business process improvement projects, but also to other operational and logistical endeavours like an office relocation.

This case study employs a waterfall project methodology, characterized by its linear, step-by-step progression. Each phase (stakeholder identification, requirement documentation, and process flow) follows sequentially, allowing for clear demarcation of tasks and responsibilities. The waterfall approach suits this project due to its well-defined, non-iterative nature.

Question Time:

1. **Stakeholder Identification**: Who are the individuals or groups that will be impacted by or have a stake in the

office move? The initial task involves identifying all relevant stakeholders, akin to the stakeholder analysis in a conventional business analysis project. Consider all the parties involved, from the relocating team members to the logistics company handling the actual move. Who might be the key stakeholders to involve from the project's start to the moving day?

2. **Engaging with Stakeholders:** Given the array of stakeholders identified, how would you devise and implement strategies to effectively manage and engage with these groups? How do you propose to communicate and address the specific needs and concerns of each stakeholder group throughout the office relocation process?

3. **Eliciting Requirements:** What specific methodologies or strategies would you utilize to gather in-depth requirements for the office relocation? How would you go about ranking or prioritizing these requirements?

4. **Requirement Documentation:** The second phase involves compiling a comprehensive list of requirements for the move. This exercise is similar to creating a Business Requirements Document (BRD) in a standard business analysis project. From physical assets that need to be moved, new equipment required, to the timeline for each step, what are all the key requirements to consider and document?

5. **Constructing a Business Requirements Document (BRD):** Could you draft a representative BRD for this

project, highlighting some of the primary requirements? What are the key sections this document should encompass and how should the requirements be presented within each section?

6. **Process Flow**: Finally, can you design a visual map of the entire relocation process? This task mirrors the creation of a Business Process Model (BPM) in a business analysis project. A BPM illustrates the workflow in a step-by-step format, easing understanding and communication. For this move, what are the sequences involved from planning, packing, transportation, setup, to post-move evaluations?

7. **Setting a Project Timeline and Milestones:** Can you design a project timeline indicating major milestones for the office relocation? What are the primary activities that need to be incorporated and when should they be scheduled?

8. **Risk Analysis:** Considering the potential for unexpected issues during a move, how would you undertake a risk assessment for this project? What could be some plausible risks, and what measures would you take to counteract them?

9. **Agile Approaches:** If you were to employ an agile methodology for this project, how might your approach diverge from a traditional one? What would be the potential benefits and obstacles of implementing an agile methodology for this project?

10. **Post-Relocation Evaluation:** Upon completion of the office relocation, how would you evaluate the success of the project? What performance measures or key performance indicators (KPIs) would you rely on?

Case Study 1: Solution

1. Stakeholder Identification

Stakeholder identification is a critical first step in any project. A stakeholder can be defined as an individual, group, or organization who has interest in or will be impacted by the outcome of a project. In the context of an office move project, there could be a wide range of stakeholders involved, both internal and external to the organization.

Here's how a business analyst might go about identifying stakeholders for the office move:

1. **Project Initiation Discussion**: The BA would typically start by having an initial discussion with the project sponsor or the person who initiated the project. They would identify key people involved in the project and ask for any necessary introductions.

2. **Identify Internal Stakeholders**: Internal stakeholders may include employees who are relocating, managers of those employees, the facilities team responsible for managing the physical aspects of the move, IT staff for relocating and setting up hardware and software systems, HR for managing the logistics and communications with the employees, and finance for tracking costs associated with the move.

3. **Identify External Stakeholders**: External stakeholders could include the moving company, real estate agents, property managers at both the current and new locations, local authorities for permits, and vendors for setting up

new services at the new location such as telecom, internet, utilities, and others.

4. **Brainstorm and Use Organization Charts**: Use company organization charts, if available, to ensure no internal groups are overlooked. Brainstorming sessions with the project team could also help identify any less obvious stakeholders.

5. **Analyze Potential Impact**: Consider who will be impacted by the move, either directly or indirectly. This may help identify stakeholders who might not be immediately obvious.

6. **Document Stakeholder Information**: For each identified stakeholder, document relevant information including their role in the project, their interest and influence level, and their key concerns and expectations from the project.

Remember, the stakeholder identification is a continuous process and can change as the project evolves. Regularly updating the stakeholder list and maintaining active communication is essential to project success.

A sample stakeholder list for this scenario could look like:

Stakeholder Name	Role/Responsibilities	Level of Involvement
Senior Management / Project Manager	Oversees the entire project, ensures successful execution	High

Stakeholder Name	Role/Responsibilities	Level of Involvement
Business Analysts	Conducts stakeholder analysis, gathers requirements	High
Current Office Employees	Will be relocated to the new office	High
New Office Employees	Will be working in the new office	High
Facilities Management Team	Manages facilities and infrastructure	High
IT Department	Handles technology and network setup	High
Human Resources	Manages employee onboarding and offboarding	High
Finance Department	Manages budget and financial aspects	High
Legal Department	Handles legal considerations and contracts	Medium
Vendors and	Provides furniture,	Medium

Stakeholder Name	Role/Responsibilities	Level of Involvement
Suppliers	equipment, and services	
Building Management (Bristol)	Coordinates move-out logistics	Medium
Building Management (Peterborough)	Coordinates move-in logistics	Medium
External Contractors	Assists with the physical move and installation	Medium
Employee Representatives	Represents employee interests and concerns	Low

2. Engaging with Stakeholders

Engaging with stakeholders is a pivotal part of any project. An effective engagement plan not only aids in smooth project execution but also ensures that the interests and concerns of all parties are addressed. For the office relocation project, the business analyst could take the following steps to engage stakeholders:

a) **Establish a Communication Plan:** Design a plan detailing when, how, and what will be communicated to each stakeholder. For example, regular status updates could be emailed to all stakeholders, while one-on-one meetings could be scheduled for decision-makers to discuss major issues or changes. The communication medium can vary based on stakeholder preference and relevance. It could range from emails, meetings, and conference calls, to more formal reports and presentations.

b) **Create Stakeholder-specific Messages:** Tailor messages according to the interests and concerns of each stakeholder group. The content, tone, and depth of information should be adjusted to fit the stakeholder. For instance, technical team members may need detailed updates on logistical matters, while executives might only require high-level status reports.

c) **Foster Open Dialogue:** Encourage stakeholders to voice their opinions and concerns. This can be achieved by creating an environment that welcomes feedback and ideas. Regular meetings, brainstorming sessions, and open-door policies can help foster this culture.

d) **Facilitate Stakeholder Involvement:** Make stakeholders feel part of the project. This could involve inviting them to project meetings, seeking their input on key decisions, or assigning them specific roles or tasks within the project.

e) **Manage Expectations:** Be transparent about what can and cannot be achieved through the project, and ensure that all stakeholders have a realistic understanding of the project's scope, timeline, and deliverables. This can help prevent misunderstandings and disappointments down the line.

Remember, stakeholder engagement is not a one-time activity but an ongoing process that should be maintained throughout the project lifecycle. Regular check-ins, updates, and adjustments should be part of the engagement strategy to ensure that all parties remain informed and involved.

3. Eliciting Requirements

In a project such as an office relocation, the business analyst's role in eliciting requirements is critical to ensure that all aspects are accounted for and planned properly. Here are a few steps that could be taken:

a) **Interviews and Discussions:** Direct interactions with stakeholders, including management, employees, and the moving company, provide firsthand information about what is required for the move. These interactions could range from formal interviews to casual conversations, and they can reveal crucial details about the requirements.

b) **Surveys and Questionnaires:** For larger teams, it might be efficient to use surveys or questionnaires to gather common requirements. They allow for reaching a broader audience in a shorter time and can help identify patterns and commonalities.

c) **Observation:** By observing current office operations, the business analyst can identify physical assets that need to be moved or might require special handling. This technique might also reveal information about potential risks or challenges.

d) **Document Analysis:** Reviewing existing documents like office layouts, asset inventories, and departmental requirements can also provide valuable insights.

e) **Workshops:** Organizing workshops with different teams can be beneficial in understanding their specific needs, addressing queries, and brainstorming potential solutions.

Once all the requirements are gathered, prioritization should be performed based on their importance to the move, their dependencies, and their impact on the project timeline and budget. Here are a few common techniques:

a) **MoSCoW Method:** This technique categorizes requirements into four categories - Must have, Should have, Could have, and Won't have. This helps in quickly identifying the non-negotiable requirements and those that can be deprioritized if needed.
b) **Value vs. Effort Matrix:** This approach involves plotting the requirements on a 2x2 grid, with one axis representing the value a requirement provides and the other representing the effort required to fulfil it. High-value, low-effort tasks are prioritized, while low-value, high-effort tasks are deprioritized.
c) **Stakeholder Voting:** Particularly useful for conflicting priorities, this democratic approach involves stakeholders voting on what they believe to be the most critical requirements.

Remember that the goal is not to fulfil all requirements but to ensure the most critical and high-value requirements are met within the constraints of time and budget.

4. **Requirements Documentation**

A business analyst would utilize a variety of techniques to elicit and document

The process of documenting the requirements for an office move is similar to creating a Business Requirements Document (BRD) in a standard business analysis project. It's vital to ensure that this document is well-structured, detailed, and comprehensible to all stakeholders involved. Here are some key considerations and steps in compiling such a document:

1. Introduction: This should outline the project's scope, including the reason for the move, key stakeholders, and the expected outcome.

2. Requirements Summary: This is a high-level overview of the main requirements. These might include the need to move certain equipment, purchase new items, or adhere to specific timelines.

3. Detailed Requirements: Each requirement should be listed and described in detail in its own section.

- **Define Business and Functional Requirements**: In an office move, business requirements could include strategic reasons for the move, budget limitations, timeline, or minimization of downtime. Functional requirements could include specific needs related to the new office space, like seating arrangements, IT setup, and accessibility needs.

- **Identify Non-Functional and Transition Requirements**: Non-functional requirements are

51

requirements that define criteria to judge the operation of a system, like ensuring minimal disruption to business operations during the move, IT systems' performance at the new office, or physical security measures at the new location. Transition requirements are the conditions that must be met to transition from the old office to the new one. This might include timelines for the move, interim workspace arrangements, equipment transport and setup, and support needed during the transition period.

These requirements could be broken down into different categories such as 'Equipment', 'Logistics', 'Personnel', 'IT', 'Legal' and 'Timeline'.

For example:

- *Equipment:* List the physical assets that need to be moved or might require special handling, new equipment that needs to be purchased, etc.

- *Logistics:* Detail the steps of the actual move, such as packing, transportation, and unloading.

- *Personnel:* Specify any changes in employee workspaces, adjustments to work schedules, or additional resources needed for the move.

- *IT:* Address the technical requirements, like transferring and setting up computer systems and internet connectivity.

- *Legal:* List any permits or approvals required for the move.

- *Timeline:* Detail when each step should happen.

.

4. Develop Use Cases or User Stories: For specific processes associated with the move, such as packing and unpacking, IT setup, or post-move support, develop use cases or user stories to outline the expected interactions between the users and the system (in this case, the process). These provide additional detail and can help ensure a smooth transition.

5. Acceptance Criteria: Define what must be done for the project to be considered successful. This might include completion within a certain timeline, minimal disruption to work, and settling into the new office without major issues.

6. Dependencies and Risks: Note any dependencies that might affect the requirements, such as needing to pack the equipment before moving it. Also, identify potential risks and how they'll be managed.

7. Prioritization: Indicate the level of importance of each requirement. Not all requirements will have the same level of priority. The document should make it clear which requirements are mandatory and which are desirable but not essential.

8. Use a Requirements Traceability Matrix: A Requirements Traceability Matrix (RTM) can be a useful tool for managing requirements throughout the project lifecycle. It helps ensure every requirement is aligned to a business need, and that it's met in the solution, tested, and delivered.

7. Document and Validate Requirements: Finally, document all gathered requirements in a structured format, often called a Business Requirement Document (BRD). Once the BRD is complete, it should be reviewed and validated with the stakeholders to ensure their requirements are accurately captured and nothing is missed.

8. Approval: Finally, have all key stakeholders sign off on the document, indicating their agreement with the documented requirements.

It's important to remember that the Business Requirements Document is not a static document; it should be reviewed and updated regularly as requirements may change or new requirements might arise during the process.

Sample **business requirements** for this scenario could look like:

Requirement ID	Requirement Description	Stakeholder	Priority
BR001	Suitable office space in Peterborough to accommodate all relocated employees	Relocating Team, Facilities Management, Senior Management	High
BR002	Reliable IT infrastructure setup	IT Department,	High

Requirement ID	Requirement Description	Stakeholder	Priority
	including workstations, servers, internet, telephones, printers	Relocating Team	
BR003	Professional moving services to ensure safe and efficient transfer of office furniture and equipment	Facilities Management, Relocating Team	High
BR004	Minimal disruption to business operations during the move	Senior Management, Relocating Team	High
BR005	Convenient location with good transport links, parking, and nearby amenities	HR, Relocating Team	Medium
BR006	Compliance with all health and safety regulations in new office	HR, Facilities Management	High

Requirement ID	Requirement Description	Stakeholder	Priority
BR007	Adequate meeting rooms, break rooms, and communal spaces in new office	Facilities Management, Relocating Team	Medium
BR008	Completion of the move within defined budget	Finance Department, Senior Management	High
BR009	Clear communication plan to keep all stakeholders informed of the move progress	HR, Senior Management	Medium
BR010	Successful negotiation of lease agreement terms for new office	Senior Management, Finance Department	Medium
BR011	Post-move support to address any issues and ensure smooth transition	IT Department, HR	Medium

Sample **functional requirements** for this scenario could look like:

Requirement ID	Requirement Description	Stakeholder	Priority
FR001	Reliable, high-speed internet connectivity to support daily business operations	IT Department, Relocating Team	High
FR002	Effective HVAC system for comfortable working conditions	Facilities Management, Relocating Team	High
FR003	Modern telecommunication systems (phones, video conferencing) to facilitate communication	IT Department, Relocating Team	High
FR004	Access control system for office security	HR, Facilities Management	High

Requirement ID	Requirement Description	Stakeholder	Priority
FR005	Adequate lighting in all areas of the office	Facilities Management, Relocating Team	Medium
FR006	Ergonomically designed workstations for all employees	HR, Facilities Management, Relocating Team	Medium
FR007	Shared network drives for team collaboration and file sharing	IT Department, Relocating Team	High
FR008	Suitable kitchen and break room facilities	Facilities Management, Relocating Team	Medium
FR009	Printing and scanning facilities accessible to all team members	IT Department, Relocating Team	Medium
FR010	Fire safety measures, including extinguishers and alarms	HR, Facilities Management	High

Requirement ID	Requirement Description	Stakeholder	Priority
FR011	Dedicated spaces for meetings and collaborations	Facilities Management, Relocating Team	Medium

Sample **non-functional requirements** for this scenario could look like:

Requirement ID	Requirement Description	Stakeholder	Priority
NFR001	Compliance with local building and safety codes in the new office	Facilities Management, HR	High
NFR002	Office should be accessible for employees with disabilities	HR, Facilities Management	High
NFR003	Office environment should adhere to ergonomic standards	HR, Facilities Management	High

Requirement ID	Requirement Description	Stakeholder	Priority
NFR004	Noise levels in work areas should be kept to a minimum to avoid distractions	HR, Facilities Management, Relocating Team	Medium
NFR005	Temperature in the office should be maintained at a comfortable level	Facilities Management, Relocating Team	Medium
NFR006	Office space should have a professional and pleasing aesthetic	Facilities Management, HR	Low
NFR007	Office should be well-lit with natural light wherever possible	Facilities Management, HR, Relocating Team	Medium
NFR008	Reliable power supply to ensure uninterrupted business operations	Facilities Management, IT Department	High

Requirement ID	Requirement Description	Stakeholder	Priority
NFR009	Sustainability standards should be maintained (e.g., waste management, energy-efficient lighting)	Facilities Management, HR	Medium
NFR010	Office layout should facilitate easy movement and collaboration among employees	Facilities Management, HR, Relocating Team	Medium

Sample **transition requirements** for this scenario could look like:

Requirement ID	Requirement Description	Stakeholder	Priority
TR001	Minimal disruption to regular business operations during the move	Senior Management, Relocating Team	High
TR002	Appropriate scheduling of move to avoid peak	Project Manager, Relocating Team	High

Requirement ID	Requirement Description	Stakeholder	Priority
	business hours		
TR003	Employees to be provided with clear instructions on the moving process	HR, Relocating Team	High
TR004	Data and IT infrastructure to be securely backed up before the move	IT Department	High
TR005	New office should be ready for move-in, including setup of IT and other equipment, before the move date	IT Department, Facilities Management	High
TR006	All services (like utilities, internet, etc.) should be functional at the new location from day one	Facilities Management, IT Department	High

Requirement ID	Requirement Description	Stakeholder	Priority
TR007	Adequate training or orientation for employees to get accustomed to the new office	HR, Relocating Team	Medium
TR008	Immediate post-move support available to address any issues or concerns	IT Department, HR, Facilities Management	Medium
TR009	A communication plan to update all stakeholders during the transition period	HR, Project Manager	Medium
TR010	Contingency plans in place to address any unexpected disruptions or delays	Project Manager, Senior Management	Medium

5. Constructing a Business Requirements Document (BRD)

Designing a visual representation or a process map of the office relocation process is an essential step that a business analyst would take

Creating a Business Requirements Document (BRD) is a key step in any project. A BRD outlines the business needs and the steps required to fulfill those needs. For this office relocation, a representative BRD might look something like this:

1. **Introduction**

   - **Purpose:** The purpose of the project, in this case, to relocate the office to a new location.

   - **Scope:** The extent of the move, including what will be moved, the departments involved, and the new location.

   - **Definitions, Acronyms, and Abbreviations:** Clarify any specific terminology or abbreviations that will be used throughout the document.

   - **References:** Mention any related documents or materials consulted or used in preparing the BRD.

   - **Overview:** Provide a brief overview of the rest of the document.

2. **Methodology**

   - Explanation of the process followed to gather and analyze the requirements.

3. **Business Requirements**

   - **High-Level Requirements:** A summary of the main business needs related to the office move.

   - **Detailed Requirements:** An in-depth exploration of each requirement. These should be broken down into various categories like 'Equipment', 'Logistics', 'Personnel', 'IT', 'Legal' and 'Timeline', detailing each requirement and its rationale.

4. **Project Timeline**

   - Detail when each step should happen and align the requirements with the respective timelines.

5. **Risk Analysis**

   - Detail any potential risks identified during the requirements gathering process, the likelihood of these risks, their potential impact, and how they can be mitigated or managed.

6. **Requirements Traceability Matrix (RTM)**

   - An RTM is a tool that helps track the project requirements throughout the project life cycle. It ensures that all requirements defined for a system are tested in the test protocols.

7. **Approvals**

   - A section for key stakeholders to sign off on the requirements.

Remember, the BRD should be written in clear, concise language so it's easily understood by all stakeholders. It should be easily accessible and reviewed and updated regularly as the project progresses. This allows any changes in requirements or business needs to be documented and tracked.

6. Process Flow

Designing a visual representation or a process map of the office relocation process is an essential step that a business analyst would take to ensure all stakeholders understand the sequence of activities involved and their respective roles.

Here are the steps a BA might follow to create this process map:

1. **Define the Scope**: The BA should first establish the boundaries of the process they are going to map. For an office relocation, this could start from the moment the decision to move was made, and end when all staff have successfully relocated and are fully operational in the new office.

2. **Identify the Steps**: Next, the BA needs to list all the necessary steps in the process. This might involve brainstorming sessions with relevant stakeholders, reviewing project documentation, or even observing how certain tasks are performed.

3. **Sequence the Steps**: Once all steps are identified, the BA needs to determine the order in which they occur. Some

tasks can be done in parallel, while others must be done sequentially. For an office relocation, steps might include procuring a moving company, packing up the old office, setting up IT infrastructure at the new office, moving furniture and equipment, unpacking and setting up the new office, and so on.

4. **Identify Key Stakeholders for Each Step**: For each step, the BA should identify who is responsible for it, who needs to be consulted, who should be informed, and who can assist in the task. This will help ensure clear communication and responsibility.

5. **Draw the Process Map**: Once the above steps are completed, the BA can begin drawing the process map. There are many tools available to create process maps, such as Microsoft Visio, Lucidchart, or even simple flowchart functions in Microsoft PowerPoint or Word. The BA should use symbols to represent the different types of activities (process, decision, data, etc.), and arrows to show the flow and sequence of these activities.

6. **Validate the Process Map**: Finally, the process map should be validated with stakeholders. This can be done in a workshop or meeting, and involves reviewing the map to ensure it accurately represents the process and that nothing has been missed.

Business Process Model and Notation (BPMN) is a global standard for graphically representing business processes in a workflow. It's used to design, visualize, execute, and control business processes, making it a valuable tool for business analysts.

A business analyst would begin by designing a high-level, or Level 0, process flow. This is also known as a context diagram and typically contains an overview of the whole process or system, its boundaries, and its interactions with external entities. The Level 0 diagram for this relocation process might include stages such as "Identify Stakeholders," "Compile Requirements," "Plan Move," "Perform Move," and "Settle into New Office."

Following the high-level view, the BA would further drill down to Level 1, 2, and so on, each providing more granular details about the processes. For instance, a Level 1 diagram of the "Plan Move" stage could include subprocesses such as "Choose Moving Company," "Prepare Current Office," and "Prepare New Office."

The BA can use BPMN elements such as flow objects (events, activities, and gateways), connecting objects, and swimlanes to represent the process flow. These elements help to depict the sequence of activities, decision points, roles involved, and the interactions among them, providing a comprehensive view of the entire relocation process.

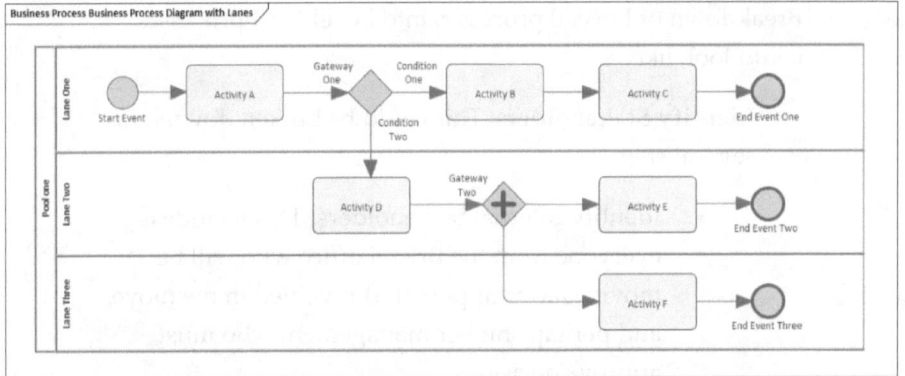

Understanding the application of BPMN and how to design different levels of process flows are crucial skills for a business analyst.

Creating a BPMN diagram for the office relocation process will not only facilitate a better understanding of the entire process but also aid in identifying potential bottlenecks, areas for improvement, and points of collaboration. The multi-level approach of the diagrams ensures that stakeholders can comprehend both the macro and micro aspects of the process.

A sample Level 0 process flow for the office move could look like:

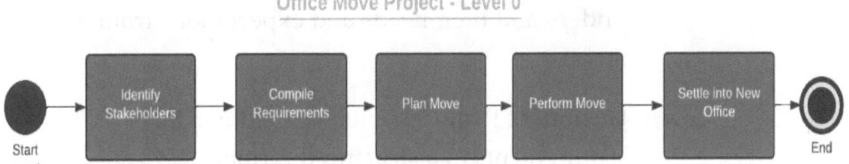

Office Move Project - Level 0

Breakdown of Level 0 processes into Level 1 subprocesses could look like:

1. **Identify Stakeholders**: This could be broken down into several steps:

    - Identify Internal Stakeholders: This includes everyone from the Bristol office who will be moving, any support staff involved in the move, and perhaps higher management who must approve decisions.

    - Identify External Stakeholders: These might include the moving company, IT service providers, office space providers, and others involved in the move.

    - Stakeholder Analysis: The BA needs to understand each stakeholder's expectations, concerns, and level of influence and interest in the project.

2. **Compile Requirements**: This could involve the following subprocesses:

    - Gather Information: Conduct interviews, workshops, and surveys with stakeholders to understand their needs and expectations from the move.

    - Document Requirements: Write down all requirements in a structured format.

- Validate Requirements: Share the requirements document with stakeholders for review and approval.

3. **Perform Move**: This could break down into steps such as:

    - Prepare Current Office: This involves packing, labelling, and preparing everything in the current office for the move.

    - Move Equipment and Personnel: The actual move, performed by the moving company.

    - Set Up New Office: Unpacking, setting up workstations, ensuring all systems are operational.

4. **Settle into New Office**: The steps could include:

    - Initial Adjustment: Address immediate concerns and issues, ensure all personnel are comfortable, all systems and processes are operational.

    - Post-Move Evaluation: Conduct a review of the move process, identify any lessons learned for future moves.

    - Ongoing Support: Address any longer-term issues that arise, ensure the new office is a productive working environment.

Each of these subprocesses in Level 1 can be further broken down into more granular steps in Level 2, Level 3, and so on, as needed. Remember, the goal of breaking down these processes is to provide a detailed understanding and manageability of the entire office move.

7. Setting a Project Timeline and Milestones

Creating a project timeline with key milestones is crucial to the success of the project. A well-defined timeline ensures that everyone involved knows their deadlines and can plan their work accordingly. Here is a sample timeline for the office relocation project:

1. **Stakeholder Identification & Requirement Gathering (Week 1-2):** Identify all relevant stakeholders and start gathering requirements from each stakeholder group.

2. **Requirement Analysis & Documentation (Week 2-3):** Analyze the collected requirements and document them in the form of a Business Requirements Document (BRD).

3. **Vendor Identification & Contract Negotiation (Week 3-5):** Identify potential vendors for moving services and negotiate contracts based on the requirements documented.

4. **Detailed Move Plan & Schedule Development (Week 6):** With a finalized list of requirements and a vendor in place, develop a detailed move plan and schedule.

5. **Packing & Pre-Move Activities (Week 7-9):** Start packing non-essential items and carry out any pre-move activities like labeling, inventorying, etc.

6. **Actual Move (Week 10):** Execute the actual move according to the schedule. This includes physically moving all items, setting up at the new location, and ensuring all IT systems are functional.

7. **Post-Move Activities (Week 11-12):** Unpack, set up all systems and spaces in the new office, troubleshoot any issues, and start normal operations.

8. **Post-Move Evaluation (Week 13):** Gather feedback from stakeholders, identify lessons learned, and document them for future reference. Evaluate the success of the project against the initial goals and objectives.

Remember, while this is a basic timeline, actual timelines may vary based on the size and complexity of the move. It's also important to build in some buffer time to manage any unexpected delays or issues that arise. All stakeholders should be kept informed about the timeline and any changes to it.

8. Risk Analysis

Risk analysis is a key component of project planning, particularly for a complex undertaking like an office relocation. Here's an outline of how you might approach risk assessment for this project:

1. Identify Potential Risks: Begin by identifying all the potential risks that could impact the office move. Some possible risks could include:

- Delay in the relocation schedule due to unexpected circumstances

- Damage to or loss of equipment during the move

- Downtime in business operations due to delayed setup

- Health and safety issues during the move

- Unforeseen costs associated with the move

- Staff resistance or low morale due to the change in location

2. Analyze and Prioritize Risks: Once you've identified potential risks, analyze each one to understand its potential impact on the project, and the likelihood of it occurring. This will help you prioritize which risks need immediate attention and which can be monitored over time.

3. Develop Risk Response Strategies: For each high-priority risk, develop a response strategy. This might include:

- Implementing additional checks and controls to prevent equipment damage or loss

- Creating a detailed move schedule and backup plans to manage potential delays

- Budgeting for unexpected costs

- Communicating clearly and frequently with staff to manage resistance and maintain morale

4. Monitor and Control Risks: Once the project is underway, continually monitor the identified risks and implement the planned response strategies as necessary. It's also important to be prepared for new risks that might emerge as the project progresses.

5. Document Lessons Learned: After the project, document the risks that occurred, how they were managed, and any lessons learned. This can be a valuable resource for managing risks in future projects.

A well-conducted risk analysis can significantly reduce the likelihood and impact of potential issues, ensuring a smoother and more successful office move.

Below is an example of a Risk Register that could be used for this office move project:

Risk ID	Risk Description	Likelihood	Impact	Risk Score (Likelihood x Impact)	Mitigation Plan
1	Delay in relocation schedule due to unexpected circumstances	3	4	12	Develop a detailed project schedule with contingency plans. Regularly monitor progress and

				adjust plans as necessary.
2	Damage to or loss of equipment during the move	2	5	10	Hire professional movers with a strong track record. Ensure equipment is properly packed and insured. Conduct an inventory before and after the move.
3	Downtime in business operations due to delayed setup	3	5	15	Plan for potential downtime in the project schedule. If possible, start setting up essential systems at the new office before the move.

4	Health and safety issues during the move	2	5	10	Ensure safety protocols are in place and followed during the move. Use professional movers to handle heavy equipment.
5	Unforeseen costs associated with the move	3	3	9	Create a detailed budget for the move, including a contingency fund for unexpected expenses. Monitor expenditures closely throughout the project.
6	Staff resistance or low morale due to change in location	2	3	6	Communicate the reasons for the move and its benefits

					clearly and frequently. Involve staff in the planning process where possible to foster buy-in and reduce resistance.

Note: Likelihood and Impact are each rated on a scale of 1 (low) to 5 (high). The Risk Score is calculated by multiplying Likelihood and Impact, providing a quantitative measure of the overall risk. This can be useful in prioritizing risk response actions.

9. Agile Approaches

Adopting an Agile methodology for an office move project, while not entirely conventional, could offer several potential benefits and present unique challenges. Agile emphasizes flexibility, collaboration, and customer satisfaction, which are all crucial to a successful office move.

In an Agile approach, the office move would be broken down into smaller, manageable parts, akin to "sprints" in Agile terminology. Each sprint could focus on a different aspect of the move such as packing, transporting, setting up the new office, etc. At the end of each sprint, the team would have a "sprint review" to discuss what went well, what could be improved, and what should be planned for the next sprint.

The key divergence between an Agile approach and a traditional project management approach, such as Waterfall, would be in its adaptive nature. While a traditional approach would try to define all requirements upfront and stick to them rigidly, Agile would allow for changes and adjustments along the way. This adaptability could be beneficial in dealing with the unexpected changes that often occur during office relocations.

Traditional Waterfall Approach:

In a traditional Waterfall project management approach, the entire office move would be planned in detail at the beginning of the project.

For example, let's assume that during the initial planning, it was decided that the IT department will be moved first. The schedule, the resources needed, the process, and other specifics would all be defined upfront. If during the execution phase, it's discovered that due to a critical project, the IT department cannot be moved as planned and the HR department should be moved first instead, this would be considered a major disruption. The entire schedule and resource allocation would need to be re-planned, causing significant delay and possibly increased costs.

This is because the Waterfall approach operates on the basis of a strict sequence of events. Deviations from this sequence can result in a cascading effect on all subsequent steps, hence the term "Waterfall".

Agile Approach:

Contrast this with an Agile approach to the same project. In Agile, you would break down the office move into smaller, manageable parts or "sprints". Each sprint might focus on moving a specific department.

Using the same scenario as above, suppose the IT department was planned to move first in Sprint 1. However, due to the same critical project, they can't move as planned. In Agile, this is less of a disruption. You can adjust the next sprint to move the HR department first.

The team holds a sprint planning meeting, revises the plan, and the project continues without significant delay or disruption. This is possible because Agile is adaptive and flexible by nature, and each sprint is planned just before it begins, allowing for such adjustments.

In summary, while Waterfall tries to anticipate and plan for every detail and possibility upfront, Agile accepts that change is inevitable and builds the flexibility to adapt into its methodology. This makes Agile particularly useful in projects where conditions are likely to change, as is often the case with office relocations.

Potential benefits of an Agile approach include:

1. **Adaptability:** Agile allows for changes in plans and requirements. If a piece of equipment is delayed or a new requirement emerges midway through the project, Agile practices allow for these changes to be incorporated smoothly.

2. **Transparency:** Regular sprint reviews and stand-up meetings ensure that all team members are aware of the project's progress, potential issues, and solutions.

3. **Risk Mitigation:** By dividing the project into sprints, you minimize the risk. If something goes wrong, it affects only one sprint, and lessons learned can be applied to the next one.

However, there could also be potential challenges:

1. **Resource Management:** Agile requires active participation from all stakeholders. If some stakeholders (e.g., senior management or external vendors) are unfamiliar with Agile or unable to commit to regular meetings and reviews, it could be difficult to follow Agile practices.

2. **Scope Creep:** Without a well-defined plan and requirements from the beginning, there's a risk that the project's scope could continually expand, leading to delays and increased costs.

3. **Time Intensive:** The regular meetings and reviews necessary in Agile could be seen as time-consuming, especially if team members are balancing their regular work with the office move.

Overall, deciding to use an Agile approach would depend on the specifics of the project and the organization's familiarity and comfort with Agile methodologies. In any case, the principles of collaboration, customer satisfaction, and iterative improvement can be beneficial to any project.

10. Post-Relocation Evaluation

Upon completion of the office relocation, it's important to evaluate the success of the project to determine whether the intended goals were achieved and to gather insights for future similar projects. The evaluation of the project's success could be based on several Key Performance Indicators (KPIs). Here are a few possible KPIs:

1. **Timeline Adherence:** One of the first and most obvious KPIs would be whether the project was completed within the defined timeline. Delays in an office move could cause disruption in normal business operations and result in additional costs. Hence, adherence to the timeline is a critical measure of success.

2. **Budget Compliance:** The next important KPI would be whether the move was accomplished within the allocated budget. Overruns could indicate issues with vendor management, estimation, or scope creep that need to be addressed.

3. **Stakeholder Satisfaction:** Stakeholder satisfaction is a crucial qualitative KPI. This could be measured through surveys or feedback sessions with different stakeholders such as employees, management, and vendors. Their feedback will provide valuable insights into what worked well and what could be improved.

4. **Business Disruption:** One of the primary goals of any office move is to ensure minimum disruption to

ongoing business activities. Metrics here could include downtime hours, the impact on productivity, or the number of business processes affected.

5. **Issue Resolution:** How effectively and efficiently issues were identified and resolved during the project is another important KPI. This could be quantified by looking at the number of issues raised and the time taken to resolve them.

6. **Asset Management:** This involves checking if all assets were properly accounted for and installed at the new location without any damage or loss.

After the relocation, a thorough review of these KPIs should be conducted to assess the overall success of the project. Lessons learned from this review should be documented and shared with the team and relevant stakeholders to improve the planning and execution of future projects. This exercise isn't just about identifying what went wrong, but also about acknowledging what went right and reinforcing those successes.

Case Study 2: Agile Project - Ecommerce Store Enhancement

Background: Welcome to a new journey, where you've joined an ecommerce team overseeing more than 700 artists' storefronts on the Shopify platform. An interesting enhancement request has arisen, with directives coming from Store Management, the specialized group responsible for designing and managing the stores via Shopify's backend.

Scenario Overview: Your initial task in this Agile project will be an important one. In line with FTC regulations, you are required to implement a functionality, where customers are mandated to check a box to acknowledge and agree to the final sale/cancellation policy, before purchasing an item marked as a final sale.

In the Agile spirit of embracing changes, the team has decided to extend this checkbox functionality to cover other aspects as well, such as:

- Acknowledgment of Pre Order Date

- Acceptance of variations in Dye Treatments (like tie dye, vinyl, etc. that might slightly differ from the image)

- Any other factors that might need explicit customer acknowledgment.

Store Management's Proposition: According to the directives from Store Management, the new checkbox section should be added either adjacent to or directly below the 'Add to Cart' button. They stress on the importance of customers not being able to progress to checkout without checking this box. If a customer tries to bypass this, an error message should be triggered: "Please review product details and agree before proceeding to checkout."

Further, a dropdown menu should be created with four options:

1. Final Sale

2. Pre Order Date

3. Dye Treatments

4. Custom

While options 1-3 will have standard wording used uniformly across all stores, option 4 will offer store operators the flexibility to craft a custom message.

The configuration for this enhancement should be accessible in the theme > theme settings > product page. This setup should allow the flexibility of enforcing the checkbox for some products while displaying only the message for others. Additionally, the presence of one of the new options should be signalled by a distinct text label or flag that appears on the slide out cart and the checkout page next to the product.

Standardized Copy for the messages:

Final Sale: *By clicking submit, you agree to our Terms and Conditions and understand that products billed as "Final Sale" or "All Sales Final" are not eligible for return, refund, or exchange.*

Pre Order Date: *By clicking submit, you are acknowledging that this product is on pre order and will ship on pre-order date provided.*

Dye Treatments *By clicking submit, you are acknowledging that the product you are purchasing is being custom dyed and therefore each unit will be slightly different in coloration.*

Proposed Solution: A potential solution put forward by the Tech Lead is the introduction of a new language key for each product type. This would be stored in Shopify's language settings, allowing a store manager to customize the messaging for each individual store. Further, a new multi-select metafield would be added, pointing to the correct language key. This is in line with Shopify's practice of using metafields to store custom data fields.

Initial mock-ups from UX designer:

Agile Project Methodology & Business Analysis Concepts: This case study is steeped in Agile Project Methodology, with a particular focus on iterative enhancements, frequent communication, and feedback loops. As a business analyst, you'll be implementing key BA concepts such as requirement elicitation, stakeholder management, crafting user stories, and possibly some UX design principles. You'll also work closely with technical team members and translate business requirements into technical language.

Question Time:

Question 1: If you were responsible for crafting user stories for this work, what questions would you pose to Store Management? What would you ask the Tech Lead or other team members?

Question 2: With the case study information provided, can you create a detailed user story? This should contain enough information for a developer to deliver the requested functionality.

Question 3: How would you structure this work from Epic to User Stories? Please provide the 'title' of the Epic and the User Stories.

Question 4: As the business analyst, how would you approach backlog prioritization for this enhancement project? What strategies or methodologies would you employ?

Question 5: What methods would you use to facilitate effective communication between the Store Management, Tech Lead, UX designer, and development team in order to promote transparency and clarity of project requirements and status?

Question 6: What role do you see the business analyst playing in the testing and acceptance phase of this enhancement? How would you define and manage the acceptance criteria?

Question 7: Given the iterative nature of Agile development, how would you, as a business analyst, ensure the continuous improvement of the solution even after its implementation?

Question 8: How would you handle changes to user stories or requirements that arise in the middle of a sprint? What is the impact of these changes and how do you communicate them to the relevant stakeholders?

Question 9: As a business analyst, how would you measure the success of this enhancement? What key performance indicators (KPIs) or other metrics would you consider?

Question 10: What Agile artifacts (like burn-down charts, sprint backlog, etc.) would you utilize in this scenario, and how would they aid you in managing and tracking the progress of the project?

Case Study 2: Solutions

In this Agile project, a Business Analyst (BA) should consider the following approach to craft user stories:

1. Understand the Business Requirements: The BA must thoroughly comprehend the project's business requirements, as outlined in the case study. This includes understanding the need for a customer acknowledgment checkbox and the different scenarios in which it should be applied (Final Sale, Pre Order Date, Dye Treatments, Custom).

2. Meet with Stakeholders: Schedule meetings with stakeholders, particularly Store Management, to discuss their needs and expectations in more depth. This could involve clarifying the placement of the checkbox, error messages, dropdown menu options, and customization capabilities.

3. Collaborate with Technical Team: It's crucial for the BA to engage in discussions with the tech lead and developers to understand the feasibility of the requirements, potential obstacles, and possible solutions.

4. Create User Stories: Following the classic format: "As a [type of user], I want [an action] so that [a benefit/a value]" can be a good starting point. Each story should be small enough to be developed, tested, and deployed within a single sprint.

The INVEST method is a highly recommended approach for writing user stories. INVEST is an acronym that stands for:

- **Independent:** Each user story should be self-contained, in a way that there is no inherent dependency on another user story. This gives you the flexibility to prioritize them in any order.

- **Negotiable:** User stories can be altered and rewritten through discussions with stakeholders and developers. They're not contracts; instead, they're invitations for a conversation.

- **Valuable:** Every user story must deliver value to the end-users and stakeholders. The value could be in the form of a new feature, an enhancement of an existing feature, or a bug fix.

- **Estimable:** A good user story can be estimated. The development team should be able to estimate the size or effort needed to develop the functionality described in the story.

- **Small:** User stories should be small enough to plan, develop, and validate within one sprint. They should not be so big that they become mini projects.

- **Testable:** Every user story should be testable. If it's difficult to figure out how to test a story, it's a sign that the story needs to be broken down further, or the requirements need to be clarified.

When applied to this case study, a potential user story could look like this: "As a customer, I want to acknowledge the final sale/cancellation policy by checking a box before adding the product to the cart, so that I am fully aware of the terms and conditions of my purchase." The story is Independent, Negotiable, Valuable to the customer, Estimable in terms of development time, Small enough to be completed in a sprint, and Testable because you can check if the acknowledgment box functionality works as expected.

5. Acceptance Criteria: Define the acceptance criteria for each user story. This helps to specify the conditions that must be met for the story to be considered 'done'. For example, in the context of this case study, an acceptance criterion for the 'Final Sale' checkbox could be: "As a customer, I should not be able to proceed to checkout without checking the 'Final Sale' acknowledgment box."

6. Prioritize User Stories: Prioritize the user stories based on the value they deliver and their dependencies.

7. Review and Validate: Review the user stories with stakeholders, get their approval, and refine the stories as necessary. This iterative feedback loop is a hallmark of Agile methodology.

8. Maintain Traceability: Keep track of the relationships between user requirements, user stories, and acceptance tests. This is helpful in understanding the impact of any future change in requirements.

Remember, the goal of a user story is to capture a high-level view of a requirement in a simple, straightforward sentence from the end user's perspective. A BA's role is to ensure that the user stories are clear, concise, and valuable to both the development team and stakeholders.

Solution to Question 1:

Following could be a set of Questions for Store Management:

1. How would you prioritize the application of these messages across your product range? Are there specific categories or products which you would like to prioritize first?

2. How frequently do you anticipate needing to change or update the messages associated with each product type?

3. For the "Custom" option, would you like to be able to create and save multiple custom messages for use across different products?

4. How would you like the system to handle instances where multiple messages might apply to a single product (e.g., a final sale item that also has a dye treatment)?

5. Would you want the ability to preview the changes made on the product page before publishing?

6. Do you have a preferred format or styling for the visual text label / flag on the slide-out cart and checkout page?

7. How often do you expect to update the "Custom" message? Should there be an approval process for updating the custom message?

8. Do you need any particular reports or analytics to track the effectiveness of this new feature?

Following could be a set of Questions for Tech Lead or other Technical Stakeholders:

1. What are the technical constraints or considerations for implementing a required checkbox and messaging system?

2. How would the metafields interact with existing data structures and how will this change affect overall performance?

3. Is it feasible to create a preview feature for Store Management to view changes before they go live?

4. How will these changes affect the mobile view of the product detail page?

5. Can we set up a process to track and report on how often customers interact with these messages or fail to check the box?

6. How would this change affect the site's overall load time, if at all?

7. What kind of testing would be required for this enhancement and how long would it take?

8. Are there any security or privacy considerations related to the storage and presentation of these messages?

9. How can we ensure that the language key change doesn't affect the functionality of other parts of the site?

10. If a product has multiple messages to show, how will the system prioritize which to display?

11. Can we implement a feature that allows for different messages to be shown at different stages in the buying process?

12. In the case of multiple languages, how will these messages be translated? Will we need to account for language translation in the metafield design?

Solution to Question 2:

Sample User Story:

As a Shopify Store Manager,

I want to have the ability to apply specific customer acknowledgement messages to different product types,

So that I can effectively communicate special conditions related to those products to customers before they proceed to checkout.

Acceptance Criteria:

1. The system should have a new section added to the product detail page, either to the right of the 'add to cart' button or directly underneath it, where a checkbox for customer acknowledgement is displayed.

2. The system should prevent customers from adding a product to their cart without checking the acknowledgement box. An error message stating "Please review product details and agree before proceeding to checkout" should be displayed if the box is not checked.

3. The system should provide a drop-down menu with four options for types of customer acknowledgement messages: "Final Sale", "Pre Order Date", "Dye Treatments", and "Custom".

4. The system should include standardized copy for the "Final Sale", "Pre Order Date", and "Dye Treatments" options, and should allow for an empty field under "Custom" where the store operator can configure a custom message.

5. The system should allow for the selection of which products the messaging applies to, and apply different messages to different products.

6. The system should add the configuration of this checkbox under theme > theme settings > product page.

7. The system should allow the option to display the messaging to the customer without a checkbox for certain products.

8. The system should display a visual text label / flag next to the product on the slide out cart and the checkout page for any products set to show one of the new options.

Technical Details:

- Tech Lead will add a new language key for each product type in Shopify's language settings. This will store the messaging and allow a store manager to modify the messaging on a store-by-store basis.

- A new multi-select metafield will be added to point to the correct language key, allowing the system to store custom fields of data.

- UX designer will provide initial mock-ups for reference.

Solution to Question 3:

Epic Title: "Shopify Theme Enhancement for Product Acknowledgement"

User Story Titles:

1. "Add New Section for Customer Acknowledgement Checkbox on Product Detail Page"

   - As a store manager, I want a dedicated section on the product detail page where customers can acknowledge understanding of product details before proceeding to checkout.

2. "Configure Acknowledgement Checkbox Functionality"

   - As a store manager, I want the system to prevent customers from adding products to the cart without checking the acknowledgement box to ensure they understand the special conditions related to the product.

3. "Implement Drop-down Menu for Acknowledgement Message Types"

   - As a store manager, I want a drop-down menu with options for standardized and custom messages, so I can choose the appropriate message type for each product.

4. "Custom Message Configuration for Store Operators"

- As a store manager, I want an option for creating and applying custom messages to products, for more flexibility in communication with customers.

5. "Product-Specific Messaging Application"

- As a store manager, I want to apply different messages to different products, so customers understand the specific conditions related to each product.

6. "Incorporate Checkbox Configuration in Theme Settings"

- As a store manager, I want to configure the acknowledgement checkbox and messaging within the theme settings of the product page for easy management.

7. "Option for Messaging without Checkbox"

- As a store manager, I want the option to display messages without a checkbox for certain products, to provide information without requiring customer acknowledgement.

8. "Visual Label Integration on Cart and Checkout Page"

- As a store manager, I want a visual text label / flag to display on the slideout cart and the checkout page for any products with special conditions, to ensure customers are reminded of the conditions before completing their purchase.

Solution to Question 4:

As a business analyst working on this enhancement project, you would use several strategies for backlog prioritization to ensure the most important and impactful work gets done first. Here's an approach one might take:

1. **Collaborate with Stakeholders**: Engage with all relevant stakeholders, including Store Management and the technical team, to understand their views on the importance of various features and requirements. This will ensure that the priorities align with the needs of both the business and the technical feasibility.

2. **Use a Prioritization Framework**: I would employ a prioritization framework like MoSCoW (Must have, Should have, Could have, Won't have), which is widely used in agile projects. This framework helps in categorizing the tasks based on their importance and urgency. For example, compliance with the FTC is a "Must have" requirement, while having a custom message could be a "Could have".

3. **Consider Business Value**: Each user story or task in the backlog delivers some value to the business. I would try to assess this value for each item, perhaps with the input of stakeholders. Those delivering higher business value would get higher priority.

4. **Evaluate Risks and Dependencies**: Some tasks may be riskier or have dependencies that need to be considered. If a high-risk item is also high-value, it might be prioritized to allow more time for dealing with any potential issues.

5. **Iterative Reevaluation**: Priorities can change as work progresses and new information becomes available. It's important to regularly reevaluate the backlog's priorities.

By implementing these strategies, we can ensure that the development team is always working on the most valuable and impactful tasks at any given time.

For prioritization, it's important to consider the immediate needs of the business, technical dependencies, and overall value. Here's a potential order of prioritization of user stories presented in Solution 3 based on the MoSCoW method, business value, and dependencies among stories:

1. "Add New Section for Customer Acknowledgement Checkbox on Product Detail Page" - As the first step in the process, this story is critical to proceed with other functionalities. It provides the basic framework for customer acknowledgement and is hence a "Must have".

2. "Configure Acknowledgement Checkbox Functionality" - This user story is crucial for compliance and customer acknowledgement before making a purchase. Therefore, it's a "Must have".

3. "Implement Drop-down Menu for Acknowledgement Message Types" - This feature is essential for selecting the right kind of message and plays a vital role in user interaction, marking it as a "Must have".

4. "Product-Specific Messaging Application" - This feature would enable customization and enhance communication

with customers. It is a "Should have" item considering its contribution to customer experience.

5. "Incorporate Checkbox Configuration in Theme Settings" - This story will streamline the management process for store managers, making it a "Should have".

6. "Custom Message Configuration for Store Operators" - This feature provides flexibility to store managers and would be a "Could have".

7. "Option for Messaging without Checkbox" - This could enhance the user experience by showing messages without requiring a checkbox interaction for certain products. This is a "Could have" as it's not strictly necessary but can enhance user experience.

8. "Visual Label Integration on Cart and Checkout Page" - This story would improve the user experience and ensure the visibility of the messages throughout the shopping process, making it a "Could have".

This prioritization focuses on functionality essential for FTC compliance and the overall shopping experience first. "Should have" and "Could have" tasks that improve the user experience and provide flexibility are prioritized next, given their importance to store managers. It's essential to re-evaluate this prioritization regularly as the project evolves.

Solution to Question 5:

Ensuring effective communication among various stakeholders is paramount in any project. Here are some methods a business analyst could employ to facilitate this:

1. **Regular Meetings:** Schedule daily standups or regular status meetings where each team member briefly shares their progress, plans for the day, and any roadblocks they are facing. This promotes transparency, unblocks team members, and keeps everyone on the same page.

2. **Product Backlog Grooming Sessions:** Hold these sessions with the Store Management, Tech Lead, UX designer, and the development team to collaboratively review, refine, and prioritize the user stories. This encourages shared understanding of the requirements and consensus on priorities.

3. **Collaborative Tools:** Leverage tools like JIRA, Trello, or Asana for project management. These tools allow everyone to see the status of various tasks and overall project progress. They also facilitate better coordination and task management.

4. **Documentation:** Clearly document the requirements, design specifications, decisions made during meetings, and any changes. Having a single source of truth helps avoid confusion and miscommunication. Tools like Confluence or Google Docs can be used for this purpose.

5. **Workshops or Brainstorming Sessions:** Hold these when starting a new feature or when facing complex problems. The goal is to harness the collective knowledge and creativity of the team.

6. **Demo Meetings:** When a piece of work is completed, the team can demo it to the stakeholders. This not only keeps everyone informed about the product's progress but also

provides an opportunity for immediate feedback and adjustments if needed.

Remember, communication isn't just about talking; it's equally about listening. Encourage everyone to voice their opinions, ideas, and concerns. This fosters an environment of trust and cooperation, which is key to successful project execution.

Solution to Question 6:

In the testing and acceptance phase of this enhancement, the Business Analyst (BA) plays an integral role in ensuring that the implemented solution aligns with the business needs and user expectations. Here's how the BA contributes to this phase:

1. **Defining Acceptance Criteria:** The BA is responsible for defining clear, specific, and measurable acceptance criteria for each user story. This criteria serves as a checklist that confirms when a story is completed and works as expected. For instance, for the user story "Configure Acknowledgement Checkbox Functionality," an acceptance criterion could be "The system prevents the addition of the product to the cart if the acknowledgement checkbox is not checked."

2. **Collaborating with the QA Team:** The BA collaborates closely with the Quality Assurance (QA) team to ensure they understand the acceptance criteria and the context behind it. This enables the QA team to create effective test

cases and validate that the developed feature meets the desired outcomes.

3. **Reviewing Test Cases:** The BA reviews the test cases prepared by the QA team to confirm they cover all aspects of the acceptance criteria. If any gaps are found, the BA suggests additions or modifications to ensure comprehensive testing.

4. **Participating in User Acceptance Testing (UAT):** In UAT, actual users test the solution in a real environment to confirm it meets their needs and works as expected. The BA often plays a role in coordinating UAT, helping define test scenarios, guiding users during testing, and collecting their feedback.

5. **Validating the Solution:** Once testing is completed, the BA validates the solution against the acceptance criteria. If the solution meets all the defined criteria, the BA approves the user story as 'Done'.

6. **Facilitating Sign-Off:** Upon completion of testing and acceptance, the BA helps in facilitating the sign-off from stakeholders, which marks the formal closure of the user story or the project.

Remember, the goal of the BA during this phase is not only to ensure the solution is implemented correctly, but also that it delivers real value to the users and the business.

Solution to Question 7:

Embracing continuous improvement is at the core of Agile development. As a Business Analyst in such an environment, there are several ways you can contribute to the ongoing refinement and enhancement of the solution post-implementation:

1. **Gather Feedback Regularly:** After implementation, continue to engage with end-users, stakeholders, and team members to gather feedback on the new functionality. Use a variety of techniques, like direct interviews, surveys, or usability testing. This feedback is invaluable in identifying areas for improvement or entirely new requirements that may emerge as users interact with the system.

2. **Review Analytics:** Analyze data and metrics relevant to the solution to understand usage patterns, user behavior, and system performance. For instance, in the ecommerce case study, metrics like how often customers interact with the acknowledgement checkbox or any increase in customer queries about products could provide valuable insights for improvement.

3. **Hold Retrospective Meetings:** Regularly scheduled retrospective meetings are a cornerstone of Agile methodology. These meetings allow the team to reflect on what worked well, what didn't, and how they can improve in the next iteration. As a BA, facilitate these discussions and encourage open dialogue about process improvement.

4. **Backlog Refinement:** Maintain and refine the product backlog by adding new user stories based on user feedback, changing business requirements, or any

insights gained from the analytics. Prioritize these backlog items in collaboration with the product owner and the team.

5. **Work Closely with the Product Owner:** Collaborate with the Product Owner to align backlog refinement with the product vision and strategy. The BA can provide essential insights from a business perspective to influence the product roadmap and the prioritization of future work.

6. **Advocate for the User:** As a BA, always ensure that the user's perspective is central to discussions about improvements or new features. This focus on user needs will help guide the development of a solution that truly provides value.

By integrating these practices into your role as a Business Analyst, you can help to cultivate a culture of continuous improvement within your Agile team. It's important to remember that improvement is a journey, not a destination - there's always room to learn and grow in Agile environments.

Solution to Question 8:

Changes in the middle of a sprint can disrupt team velocity and workflow. However, Agile methodology is designed to accommodate change, so there are ways to manage such situations effectively.

1. **Evaluate the Change:** First, it's important to assess the necessity and urgency of the change. If the change is crucial and cannot wait until the next sprint, then consider bringing it to the team's attention. However, if

the change can wait, it's often best to avoid disrupting the current sprint and instead add the new or modified user story to the backlog for prioritization in a future sprint.

2. **Discuss with the Product Owner:** Any significant change should first be discussed with the Product Owner. They are responsible for the product backlog and have the final say on whether a change should be included in the current sprint or deferred to a later sprint.

3. **Communicate with the Team:** If a change is to be introduced in the current sprint, discuss it openly with the development team. Review the impact it may have on their current work, and consider if tasks need to be re-prioritized or if the sprint goal will need to be adjusted.

4. **Re-prioritize User Stories:** If the change is accepted within the current sprint, re-prioritize the user stories in the sprint backlog. It may be necessary to remove a user story of equivalent effort to accommodate the new requirement, to prevent overloading the team and jeopardizing sprint goals.

5. **Inform Stakeholders:** Once the decision is made, promptly communicate it to all relevant stakeholders. Transparency is key in Agile and stakeholders need to be aware of changes that could potentially affect the project's timeline or output.

6. **Inspect and Adapt:** After the sprint, during the retrospective meeting, discuss the impact of the mid-sprint change. This is an opportunity to learn and

improve your team's approach to handling such changes in the future.

Remember, the goal of Agile is to deliver value to the end user quickly and frequently. Sometimes, accommodating changes within the sprint aligns more with this objective than rigidly sticking to the planned user stories. However, it is a delicate balance and must be handled carefully to prevent frequent disruptions and ensure the team can still deliver on its commitments.

Solution to Question 9:

Success measurement is a critical part of any project or enhancement, as it provides a clear indication of how well the solution is working and whether it is delivering the expected value. As a business analyst, you would typically consider a variety of quantitative and qualitative measures to gauge success. Here's how you might approach it for this eCommerce store enhancement:

1. **User Adoption Rate:** Measure the percentage of users who are successfully utilizing the new functionality compared to the total number of users. This provides a clear indicator of whether the feature is being used and, by extension, if it is useful to the customers.

2. **Number of Transactions Without Errors or Support Requests:** Monitor the number of transactions that are completed successfully without any system errors or requiring any support assistance. This can help identify if the new feature is working as intended and providing a smooth user experience.

3. **Reduction in Customer Support Queries:** One of the goals of the enhancement is to ensure customers are fully aware of the conditions related to certain products before making a purchase. This should ideally lead to fewer queries or complaints about these conditions, which can be measured by tracking the volume of related customer support requests.

4. **Sales Conversion Rate:** Analyze if there's any increase in the sales conversion rate post-implementation. If the new feature is enhancing customer understanding and confidence, it might positively impact sales.

5. **Customer Feedback:** Qualitative measures such as customer feedback and reviews can also be a good way to gauge how well the new feature is received. This can be collected through surveys, social media, or direct customer feedback.

6. **Abandoned Cart Rate:** Track any changes in the rate of cart abandonment. If the feature is not designed or implemented properly, it might confuse or frustrate customers and lead to an increase in abandoned carts.

Remember, the selection of KPIs and other metrics will depend on the specific objectives of the enhancement and the wider goals of the business. It's important to choose those that align with these goals and provide a meaningful measure of success. Always review and analyze these metrics over time, and use this insight to drive continuous improvement.

Solution to Question 10:

In an Agile environment, several artifacts can be useful in managing and tracking the progress of the project. Here are some examples and how they might be applied to this eCommerce store enhancement:

1. **Product Backlog:** This is a prioritized list of features (user stories or epics) that need to be developed for the product. For this case, the product backlog would include the user stories related to the new checkbox feature on the product detail page, along with any other enhancements or features that are planned for the eCommerce store. It serves as a guide for what work needs to be done.

2. **Sprint Backlog:** This is a subset of the product backlog, and it contains the user stories that the team has committed to working on during the current sprint. In this case, it might include user stories like "Add New Section for Customer Acknowledgement Checkbox on Product Detail Page" and "Configure Acknowledgement Checkbox Functionality". The sprint backlog provides a clear overview of the work planned for the current sprint.

3. **Burn-down Charts:** A burn-down chart is a graphical representation of work left to do versus time. It helps to visualize the amount of work completed and the amount remaining over time, allowing you to track if the project is on schedule. In this scenario, a burn-down chart could be used to monitor progress on the user stories related to the new checkbox feature.

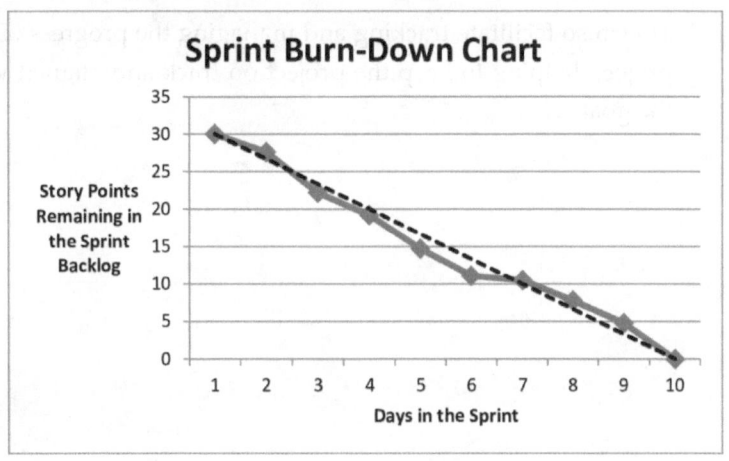

Sprint Burn-Down Chart

4. **User Story Map:** This is a visual representation of the product backlog, which helps to understand the user journey and how the different user stories fit together. In this context, a user story map would provide an overview of how the different elements of the new checkbox feature fit into the overall user journey on the eCommerce store.

5. **Definition of Done (DoD):** This artifact outlines the criteria a user story or task must meet to be considered complete. This provides clear guidance to the development team and helps ensure quality and consistency in the completed work.

6. **Product Increment:** This is the sum of all product backlog items completed during a sprint. For this case, it could include a working version of the checkbox feature, ready to be reviewed and tested.

These artifacts help to ensure transparency and foster better communication, both within the team and with stakeholders.

They also facilitate tracking and managing the progress of the project, helping to keep the project on track and aligned with the goals.

Case Study 3: Evaluating Business Strategy at ABC Plastics

ABC Plastics is a multinational corporation specializing in the manufacture and distribution of a diverse array of plastic products. The company has a global footprint with manufacturing bases located in China and Australia, sales management centred in North America, and support functions stationed in the UK. Despite its wide-ranging operations, the organization's board is keen on exploring avenues for further expansion.

The board has tabled two proposals for consideration: The first idea involves introducing a new product utilizing the existing distribution network. The second proposal calls for the expansion of the company's distribution network into a geographical region that currently falls outside their operational purview.

You are a Business Analyst (BA) based in the UK, working closely with the Change Controller, who has not yet been assigned. As a BA, your immediate task is to shape the project and prepare it for a seamless transition to the Change Controller once assigned. As you contemplate this, bear in mind the time differences with your global teams: Sydney is 9 hours ahead and Washington D.C is 5 hours behind UK time.

This case study engages several business analyst concepts including strategic analysis, stakeholder management, requirements elicitation and documentation, creation of a

Business Requirements Document (BRD), and navigating organizational change.

The primary project methodology underpinning this case study is a traditional Waterfall approach, given its sequential stages align with the needs of the case. However, Agile elements could be incorporated as needed, especially when dealing with changes and iterations based on stakeholder feedback.

Question Time

1. **Strategic Analysis:** Based on the information provided, provide an analysis on which proposal – introducing a new product or expanding into a new geographical region – might better serve the business. Be sure to identify and state your assumptions where appropriate.

2. **Initiation Documentation:** As a BA tasked with shaping the project, what documents would you produce to facilitate a smooth transition to the Change Controller?

3. **Ongoing Documentation:** Once the project is underway, what documents will you, as the BA, produce throughout the lifecycle of the project to ensure clear communication and project tracking?

4. **Requirements Elicitation:** How would you gather the necessary requirements to produce an effective BRD? Describe the techniques you would use to elicit the requirements and how you would triage and manage them.

5. **Stakeholder Management:** What stakeholder management techniques would you employ to ensure clear communication and collaboration among the various global teams involved in this project?

6. **Unexpected Stakeholder Scenario:** Imagine you discover that the R&D department at the Australian site, who were not involved in the initial requirements gathering, have independently developed a prototype of the new product and are about to start market feedback. They are reluctant to be involved with the project and perceive your involvement as an interference, having executed similar tasks without external help before. How would you integrate them into the stakeholders group and align them with the project's goals, especially in the absence of a designated Change Controller?

Case Study 3: Solutions

Solution 1: Strategic Analysis

Based on the scenario, there are two potential strategies for expansion:

1. Introduce a new product through existing distribution channels.

2. Expand their distribution network to a new geographic region.

To determine which of the two would be a better solution, we would conduct a thorough analysis using factors such as market research, financial implications, and operational capacity.

Let's conduct a brief analysis.

1. Introducing a new product through existing distribution channels:

Assumptions:

- ABC Plastics already has a successful and efficient distribution channel in place.

- The new product is relevant to the current market segment and meets a current or future need.

Pros:

- Utilize existing relationships with distribution partners.

- Lower cost as compared to geographical expansion.

- Faster implementation as the company already knows the existing market.

Cons:

- Dependence on the success of the new product.

- If the new product fails, it could have negative repercussions on the existing product line.

- Can lead to market saturation if the new product is similar to existing ones.

2. Expanding the distribution network to a new geographic region:

Assumptions:

- There is a demand for ABC Plastics' products in the new geographical region.

- The company has the resources and capabilities to manage the logistical challenges associated with geographical expansion.

Pros:

- Access to a new market, potentially increasing revenue.

- Diversification of business risk across different markets.

- Potential for capturing more market share and establishing the brand more widely.

Cons:

- Requires significant investment and resources.

117

- Potential legal and cultural barriers to entry.

- Increased complexity in operations and supply chain management.

Financial Implication Analysis:

A detailed financial analysis should be conducted to determine the costs associated with each option and compare them against the projected revenues. This should include a break-even analysis and a return on investment calculation.

Operational Capacity Analysis:

ABC Plastics must analyze its current operational capacity. For a new product, do they have the capacity to manufacture it? If not, what would be the cost of increasing capacity? For geographical expansion, do they have the capacity to produce enough products to meet the demand in the new market?

In conclusion, the final decision should be based on the combination of market research data, financial implications, and operational capacity analysis, along with the company's long-term strategic goals. It is important to note that these decisions are not mutually exclusive; ABC Plastics could choose to implement both strategies over a longer timeline, thus maximizing potential growth. However, further data and research are needed to come to a solid conclusion.

Once the analysis is complete, it would be easier to provide a specific recommendation on whether introducing a new product or expanding to a new geographic region would be more beneficial to ABC Plastics.

This initial analysis is subject to revision based on additional data or changes in business conditions.

Solution 2: Initiation Documentation

A Business Analyst would prepare comprehensive documents that would help the Change Controller to understand the project completely and take it forward effectively. Here are the key documents that would be produced:

1. Project Scope Document: This document would include detailed information about the project's objectives, deliverables, milestones, timelines, and budget. It would also clarify what's out of scope to prevent scope creep.

2. Business Requirements Document (BRD): This document would detail the business needs and expectations, justifying the project. It would include the functionality required from a business standpoint, key performance indicators (KPIs), and business processes.

3. Stakeholder Analysis: This document identifies all the key stakeholders involved in the project, their roles, interests, and level of influence.

4. Market Analysis Report: This includes all findings from the market research done to assess the feasibility of the new product or new market expansion.

5. Risk Assessment and Mitigation Plan: This document identifies potential risks associated with the project and outlines the steps to mitigate them.

6. Project Communication Plan: This outlines who needs to be communicated with, when, how, and what information needs to be shared.

7. Functional Specifications Document (FSD): It translates the business requirements into technical terms that can be implemented by the IT/development team.

8. Change Management Plan: This would outline how changes to the project will be managed, including how changes are approved and documented.

9. Resource Allocation Plan: A document showing which resources are assigned to the project, their responsibilities, and when and how they will be utilised.

10. Project Handover Document: This document includes a summary of all documents, resources, current project status, outstanding items, next steps, key contact information, etc., so the Change Controller can easily transition into the project.

These documents will be living documents that evolve with the project. They would be shared with the Change Controller and other key stakeholders, ensuring everyone is aligned and understands their responsibilities. This will allow for an easier transition and help the Change Controller 'hit the ground running'.

Solution 3: Ongoing Documentation

A Business Analyst (BA) would produce several key documents throughout the lifetime of the project to ensure smooth operation, effective communication, and continuous alignment with project goals. Here are some of the essential documents:

1. Project Status Reports: Regular updates regarding the project's progress, detailing what has been accomplished, any issues encountered, and the upcoming tasks. It helps keep stakeholders informed about the project's current state.

2. Requirements Traceability Matrix (RTM): This document is used to track requirements during the project's life cycle. It helps ensure that all requirements are met and links them to their source and output.

3. Updated Project Plan: The project plan is a living document and will need to be updated as the project progresses to reflect changes and keep track of the project timeline and milestones.

4. Change Request Forms: Any changes in scope, timelines, resources, etc., are documented using change request forms, which are then approved as per the Change Management Plan.

5. Risk Register: A document to track identified risks and their status. The risk register is continuously updated throughout the project.

6. Meeting Minutes: Documentation of all meetings, including decisions made, action items, and responsibilities assigned.

7. Updated Risk Assessment and Mitigation Plan: The Risk Assessment and Mitigation Plan will be updated continuously as new risks can come up, or old risks may change or be eliminated.

8. Lessons Learned Document: Throughout the project, this document is used to track challenges faced, solutions implemented, and lessons learned for future reference.

9. User Stories or Use Cases: If the project involves developing a new system or software, the BA will create user stories or use cases to help the development team understand how end-users will interact with the system.

10. Test Cases: The BA will develop test cases based on the requirements to ensure that the solution meets the business needs.

11. Business Process Models: These are diagrams that depict the current (as-is) and future (to-be) state of the business processes.

All these documents play a crucial role in ensuring that the project runs smoothly, stays aligned with business objectives, meets the requirements as expected, and manages risks effectively. The BA will ensure these documents are updated as the project evolves and are available to relevant stakeholders for transparency and smooth project execution.

Solution 4: Requirements Elicitation

Gathering requirements to produce a comprehensive Business Requirements Document (BRD) is a critical step in any project. There are several techniques to elicit requirements:

1. Interviews: Conducting one-on-one or group interviews with stakeholders, including management, project sponsors, end-users, or other relevant individuals. These interviews can provide a wealth of information about business needs and expectations.

2. Workshops: Organizing workshops with various stakeholders can encourage discussions and brainstorming, leading to a clearer understanding of business needs and potential solutions.

3. Surveys and Questionnaires: These can be used when you need to gather data from a large number of people. They're especially useful for gathering user requirements or identifying common problems that need to be addressed.

4. Document Analysis: Reviewing existing documentation related to the business process can provide insights into current processes and identify areas for improvement.

5. Observation: Sometimes, the best way to understand a process or a problem is to observe it in action. Watching end-users interact with a system can identify pain points that might not come up in interviews or surveys.

6. Prototyping: Creating a preliminary model of the new system or process can help stakeholders visualize the end product and provide feedback on its functionality.

Once the requirements have been gathered, they need to be analyzed, documented, and managed. Here are some steps to do that:

Requirement Triage and Management:

1. Categorization: Group the requirements based on their type, such as functional, non-functional, technical, etc. This will help in prioritizing and managing them more effectively.

2. Prioritization: All requirements are not equal. Some are must-haves while others could be nice-to-haves. Techniques such as the MoSCoW method (Must have, Should have, Could have, and Won't have) can be used for prioritization.

3. Documentation: All requirements should be documented in the BRD along with their sources. This includes the rationale behind each requirement, any assumptions made, and the expected outcome.

4. Validation: Ensure the documented requirements are reviewed and validated by the stakeholders. This will confirm that all requirements are accurate, complete, and in alignment with business goals.

5. Management: Use a Requirements Traceability Matrix (RTM) to track the status of each requirement throughout the project. This can help ensure that all requirements are met and can provide a reference for any changes or updates.

6. Change Control: Any changes to the requirements should be controlled and documented using a change control process. This includes logging the change request, evaluating its impact, making a decision, and updating the BRD and RTM accordingly.

By diligently following these steps, you can ensure that the project is based on well-defined, agreed-upon requirements and that it remains aligned with these requirements throughout its life cycle.

Solution 5: Stakeholder Management

Stakeholder management is crucial for the success of any project. Here are some of the stakeholder management techniques that a Business Analyst would employ for this project:

1. Stakeholder Identification:

Identify all the stakeholders involved in the project. These might include board members, project team members, end-users, and other people affected by the project. It could also include external stakeholders like suppliers, regulators, or customers.

2. Stakeholder Analysis:

Conduct a stakeholder analysis to understand the interests, influence, and expectations of each stakeholder. Tools like the power/interest grid can help categorize stakeholders based on their power over the project and their interest in the project outcomes.

3. Stakeholder Communication Plan:

Create a communication plan tailored to each stakeholder group. This plan would outline who will communicate what information to whom, when, and through what channel. Ensure that the communication is clear, concise, and relevant to the stakeholder.

4. Stakeholder Engagement:

125

Engage stakeholders throughout the project lifecycle. This could involve regular meetings, workshops, or status updates. The aim is to keep stakeholders involved and invested in the project's success.

5. Managing Stakeholder Expectations:

Set realistic expectations and keep stakeholders informed about the project's progress and any changes. This helps to ensure that all stakeholders have a clear understanding of what the project will deliver and when.

6. Conflict Management:

Conflicts can arise during a project, particularly between stakeholders with different interests or goals. It's important to address these conflicts as soon as they arise, using negotiation or mediation techniques.

7. Stakeholder Feedback:

Regularly solicit feedback from stakeholders. This can provide valuable insights into the project's performance and identify areas for improvement. Feedback can also be used to assess stakeholder satisfaction and make adjustments as needed.

By applying these stakeholder management techniques, it's possible to ensure that all stakeholders remain engaged and supportive of the project, ultimately contributing to its success.

Solution 6: Unexpected Stakeholder Scenario

Navigating such a situation requires diplomacy, communication, and inclusion. Here are the steps a Business Analyst would take to incorporate the Australian site R&D department into the project:

1. Acknowledge Their Expertise:

Firstly, I would acknowledge their work, expertise, and past successes. Express genuine interest in the prototype they have developed and their market feedback initiatives.

2. Communicate the Project Vision and Goals:

I would clearly communicate the project's overarching goals, explaining how it aligns with the organization's broader objectives. It's essential to convey that ones role as a BA is not to interfere but to facilitate and ensure alignment between all stakeholders and project goals.

3. Involve them in Decision-Making Process:

Engage them in project meetings and decision-making processes. By giving them a voice and a sense of ownership, they will feel more involved and less like the project is being imposed on them.

4. Clarify Roles:

Establish clear roles and responsibilities. Explain that their expertise in prototyping and gathering market feedback is critical to the project, but other aspects need to be managed as well to ensure project success.

5. Establish Regular Communication:

Given the time zone differences, it's important to find mutually convenient times for regular updates and check-ins. Use these sessions not just for updates but also to build rapport and trust.

6. Highlight the Benefits:

Highlight the benefits they stand to gain from this project, such as additional resources, a broader perspective, or a more coordinated approach to launching the new product.

7. Leverage Senior Management:

If they remain hesitant, it might be helpful to have a senior executive reinforce the importance of the project and their participation in it. This can signal that the project has organization-wide importance and is not merely an external imposition.

By adopting a respectful, inclusive approach and maintaining open lines of communication, you can hopefully win their trust and cooperation, aligning them with the project's objectives and creating a more cohesive, effective project team.

Case Study 4: Enhancing Operational Efficiency with AI at TfL London

As a Business Analyst, you've been tasked with an integral project at Transport for London (TfL). The goal is to enhance the efficiency and effectiveness of the London bus network, a project deemed of high significance due to the mounting strains on the transport system. This pressure stems from a burgeoning population and the crucial need to mitigate carbon emissions.

TfL is in possession of an extensive range of data including:

- GPS data from buses, tracking their speed, location, and timings.

- Ticketing data, providing insights into passenger load at different times and across different routes.

- Customer feedback and complaints data.

- Traffic congestion data in London.

- Data from a recent survey on passenger travel patterns and preferences.

However, TfL has been grappling with a few challenges:

- Overcrowding on buses during peak hours and low passenger presence during off-peak hours.

- Frequent delays on some bus routes due to traffic congestion.

- Concerns regarding the carbon footprint of the bus network.

- Financial strain to maintain cost-effectiveness of the bus network.

As a potential solution, TfL is contemplating the implementation of a new AI-based tool. This tool is designed to optimize bus scheduling and reduce the carbon footprint by utilizing various datasets like GPS data, passenger load data, and traffic congestion data. The introduction of this tool may result in alterations to the existing bus schedules and routes, influencing a wide range of stakeholders, including passengers, bus drivers, and local communities.

This case study applies several business analyst concepts such as problem-solving, decision making, planning and organization, stakeholder communication, and influence. It also leverages AI and data analysis to enhance operational efficiency. The project methodology is a hybrid one, combining elements of Waterfall (for well-defined tasks like data collection and tool implementation) and Agile (for iterative tasks like stakeholder communication, testing, and improvements).

Question:

As a Business Analyst, how would you navigate this scenario? Your answer should detail your approach in terms of planning and organizing your work, communicating with and influencing various stakeholders, problem-solving and decision-making in the face of potential challenges. It should also highlight how you would maintain a robust focus on achieving the desired outcomes of improved bus scheduling and reduced carbon footprint.

Case Study 4: Solution

In order to address the challenges and effectively capitalize on the potential of the new AI-based tool, a multifaceted and strategic approach is needed.

First and foremost, the capabilities and requirements of the AI tool must be fully understood. This requires close collaboration with the tool's technical team to gather the necessary insights and anticipate potential impacts.

The next critical step is to create a detailed project plan. This plan should include clear objectives, deadlines, and defined responsibilities, encompassing all aspects of the project - from data analysis and stakeholder consultation to solution implementation and post-implementation review.

Decision-making should be driven by data. By analysing available datasets such as GPS data, passenger load data, and traffic congestion data, potential implications of the AI tool on bus schedules and routes can be anticipated.

Stakeholder management plays a crucial role in the success of this project. Identifying all key stakeholders, which include passengers, bus drivers, and local communities, and seeking their feedback early in the process can help to align their expectations with the project's objectives, thereby mitigating potential resistance and securing stakeholder buy-in.

A problem-solving mindset should be adopted to anticipate and address potential challenges. For example, if significant passenger inconvenience is anticipated due to changes proposed by the AI tool, there is a need to find a balance

132

between improved efficiency, reduced carbon footprint, and passenger satisfaction. This might involve working with the technical team to tweak the tool's algorithms or parameters to minimize disruption while achieving the intended environmental benefits.

In terms of communication, transparency and regular updates to all stakeholders are key. This might include presentations to explain how the AI tool works, what benefits are expected, and how stakeholder feedback is being incorporated. These actions can help convince stakeholders of the project's benefits and reassure them that their concerns are being addressed.

Lastly, a strong focus on the desired outcomes - improved bus scheduling and reduced carbon footprint - is vital. Progress against these objectives should be regularly monitored and evaluated, with Key Performance Indicators (KPIs) and a regular reporting system set up. After implementation, feedback should be gathered and outcomes monitored to enable continuous improvements.

In conclusion, this comprehensive approach harnesses key competencies such as planning & organising, communication & influence, problem-solving & decision-making, results focus, and stakeholder management, to steer the project towards success.

Case Study 5: App Feature Development for Order Management Efficiency

Context

Swiggy, a food delivery giant, aims to introduce an innovative approach to manage their order assignments for Delivery Managers. The goal is to optimize the utilization of delivery resources and ensure seamless operation across various demand periods.

Problem Statement

The primary issue is to enhance delivery efficiency using the existing workforce. The challenges are two-fold:

1. During peak demand (lunch and dinner times), orders increase significantly. The goal here is to maximize the number of customers served by the same set of Delivery Boys.

2. During off-peak hours, it's essential to keep all Delivery Boys engaged without overburdening specific individuals.

Proposed Solution

To address these challenges, an intelligent assignment system with two distinct flags, 'peak hours' and 'off-peak hours,' is proposed. This system would enable an optimized allocation logic during peak hours (allowing a single Delivery Boy to handle multiple orders on similar routes) and ensure even distribution of work during off-peak hours via a round-robin approach. Furthermore, the introduction of a configurable dashboard will automate the rule settings based on time and day, reducing manual intervention.

Question:

In this case study, as a Business Analyst you are tasked with producing the **Feature Requirement Document (FRD)**. This document would elucidate the objectives of the Delivery Manager, including monitoring the current order assignment configuration, altering assignment rules, and visualizing real-time order allocation. Key components of this document include user stories, user flows, and acceptance criteria, all of which are vital requirements elicitation techniques. Wireframes or prototypes, serving as visual aids, can further enhance understanding and stakeholder buy-in.

The primary project methodology followed in this case study leans towards an agile approach, given the need for fast iteration and the inclusion of user stories. Furthermore, the development of wireframes or prototypes for validation indicates a user-centred design approach.

It's worth noting that the focus of these deliverables is to provide functional outputs and user-friendly interfaces. The technical implementation, including coding, is the responsibility of the respective tech teams, highlighting the collaborative nature of a Business Analyst's role in a project.

Case Study 5: Solution

Feature Requirements Document

Introduction

This document outlines the feature requirements for the Delivery Boy Assignment Logic system for the backend portal used by delivery managers at Swiggy. It provides a detailed description of the system functionality, including user stories, user flows, and acceptance criteria.

Feature Description

The proposed system will offer dynamic delivery assignment logic that can be configured to optimize order allocation based on time of day and delivery boy availability. It will contain a visual dashboard that allows delivery managers to set configurations and monitor the effectiveness of the set rules.

User Stories and Acceptance Criteria

User Story 1:

As a Delivery Manager, I want to view the current order assignment configuration so that I can understand how the orders are being assigned.

Acceptance Criteria:

The backend portal displays the current order assignment configuration.

The configuration includes the flags for peak hours, off-peak hours, and non-working hours.

The configuration clearly indicates the logic being applied during different time periods.

User Flow:

The Delivery Manager opens the backend portal.

The portal displays the current order assignment configuration, including the flags set for peak hours, off-peak hours, and non-working hours.

The manager can view the current logic being applied for order assignment during different time periods.

Use Story 2:

As a Delivery Manager, I want to change the assignment rules based on different scenarios such as peak hours, off-peak hours, and non-working hours so that I can optimize the delivery assignments.

Acceptance Criteria:

The frontend app provides a configuration settings page.

The settings page allows the manager to set the flags for peak hours, off-peak hours, and non-working hours.

The manager can specify the logic to be applied during peak hours, such as allocating multiple orders to each delivery boy.

The manager can specify the logic to be applied during off-peak hours, such as assigning orders sequentially in a round-robin fashion.

The manager can define rules for non-working hours to ensure no orders are assigned during that time.

User Flow:

The Delivery Manager accesses the configuration settings page in the frontend app.

The configuration settings page allows the manager to set the flags for peak hours, off-peak hours, and non-working hours.

The manager can specify the logic to be applied during peak hours and off-peak hours, such as allocating multiple orders to each delivery boy or assigning orders sequentially in a round-robin fashion.

The manager can set the rules for non-working hours, ensuring that no orders are assigned during that time.

Use Story 3: As a Delivery Manager, I want to verify if the active deliveries have been assigned to delivery boys according to the configured rules so that I can ensure the correct assignments are made.

Acceptance Criteria:

The frontend app includes an active deliveries page.

The page displays the currently active deliveries.

The page shows the delivery boys assigned to each order.

The manager can easily compare the assigned deliveries with the configured rules to verify if they align correctly.

User Flow:

The Delivery Manager accesses the active deliveries page in the frontend app.

The page displays the currently active deliveries and the delivery boys assigned to each order.

The manager can check if the assignment of deliveries aligns with the configured rules and logic.

Frontend App Page

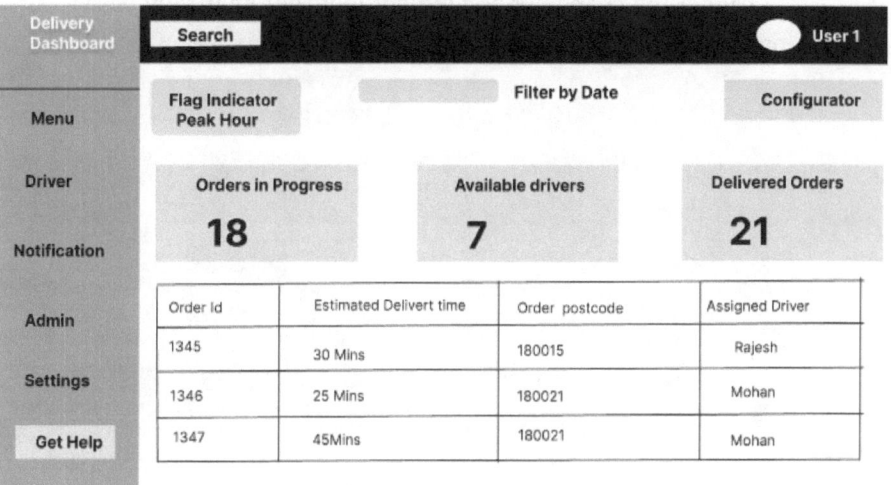

Frontend and Backend Guidelines

The frontend will contain an interactive dashboard for viewing and modifying delivery assignment rules. This dashboard should display the current rule, the schedule for upcoming rules, and a list of all delivery boys and their current assignments. The frontend should also have an intuitive interface for modifying the schedule.

The backend should contain the logic for assigning orders based on the current rule and time of day. It should also provide APIs for the frontend to retrieve and modify assignment rules and schedules.

The backend should also contain a configuration system for defining the rules and schedules. This system should be able to trigger the change of assignment logic automatically based on the current time and configured schedule.

Case Study 6: Promoting Labor Market Inclusion for People of Determination (PoDs)

Context

In the UAE, legislative measures have been instituted to protect and empower People of Determination (PoDs), known globally as people with disabilities. Despite these legal frameworks, such as the Federal Law No. 43 of 2018, the practical implementation lags, resulting in widespread unemployment among PoDs.

Problem Statement

The issue at hand revolves around the under-utilization of PoDs in the labor market, with over 90% of Emiratis with disabilities unemployed as of 2019. There's a gap between the legal provisions and their enforcement, leading to this significant societal challenge.

Goals

1. **Benchmark Analysis**: Conduct a thorough analysis of best-in-class global benchmarks on the labor market inclusion and empowerment of PoDs. This research would involve investigating successful cases worldwide, studying their methods, implementation, and outcomes to draw actionable insights.

2. **Recommend Measures**: Develop a set of comprehensive recommendations to support and include PoDs in the labor market. These could range from policy reforms,

legislative enhancements, incentives to employers, to targeted employment programs for PoDs.

In this case study, a Business Analyst would leverage various skills and methodologies:

Benchmarking and Comparative Analysis: This involves comparing UAE's situation with successful cases globally. It's not just about statistics but also understanding the socio-cultural, economic, and legislative factors contributing to successful outcomes.

Requirements Elicitation and Analysis: The BA would need to understand the current situation in-depth, the challenges faced by PoDs in securing employment, and the limitations in existing laws and policies. This could involve interviews, focus groups, and surveys.

Stakeholder Analysis and Management: The BA would identify and work with various stakeholders, including government bodies, non-profit organizations, PoDs themselves, and potential employers.

Policy Analysis and Development: Based on the findings, the BA would suggest improvements in current laws and policies, propose new ones if necessary, and identify potential incentives for employers to hire PoDs.

Strategy Formulation: Apart from policies and laws, the BA might propose targeted programs for skill development, vocational training, and employer awareness. This would involve strategic planning and program management.

The approach adopted in this case study aligns with the broader goals of **Business Analysis** - understanding the problem, gathering and analyzing information, and proposing actionable solutions. It also demonstrates the wide-ranging roles of a BA, from research and analysis to policy development and strategic planning.

Case Study 6 Solution:

Below is a suggested Business Analysis approach to tackle the problem in the case study:

Step 1: Benchmark Analysis Initiate the project with an in-depth study of international standards for labor market inclusion and empowerment of PoDs. The objective is to identify successful strategies, regulations, and incentives that have effectively promoted the employment of PoDs.

- **Legislative Review**: Examine legislations such as the Americans with Disabilities Act (ADA) in the United States and the Equality Act in the UK that mandate non-discrimination in the employment of individuals with disabilities. These serve as practical templates for effective regulatory frameworks.

- **Incentive Schemes**: Investigate the different incentives offered to organizations to promote PoDs' hiring, which might include tax benefits, subsidies, or public recognition initiatives.

- **Workplace Accommodations**: Understand how the adoption of physical and digital accommodations enables PoDs to perform efficiently. Examples include accessibility features, assistive technologies, and flexible work schedules.

- **Education and Training Programs**: Identify training initiatives aimed at equipping PoDs with the skills and qualifications necessary for various employment opportunities.

144

Step 2: Tailored Recommendations for the UAE Leveraging the insights from benchmark analysis, develop a set of tailored measures that consider the UAE's unique cultural, economic, and societal context:

- **Legislative Enhancements**: Propose amendments to existing laws or suggest new ones that strengthen labor market protections and support for PoDs.

- **Employer Incentives**: Recommend incentives, such as tax benefits or subsidies, to stimulate UAE businesses' interest in hiring and supporting PoDs.

- **Law Enforcement**: Outline strategies to improve the enforcement of existing laws. This could encompass penalties for non-compliance or robust reporting and oversight mechanisms.

- **Promoting Workplace Accommodations and Assistive Technologies**: Advocate for measures that boost workplace accessibility and encourage the use of assistive technologies.

- **Expanding Education and Training Opportunities**: Propose the establishment or expansion of programs aimed at equipping PoDs with necessary skills and qualifications.

In conclusion, this problem-solving approach exemplifies the core competencies of Business Analysis: identifying and understanding the problem, researching and analyzing comparative data, and developing strategic recommendations based on the analysis.

Case Study 7: Streamlining Invoice Processing Through Automation

In this case study, the need for automation in invoice processing is presented. Here, you'll take the role of a business analyst, called upon by the Project Manager, Peter Slack. The business goal is clear: develop an automated system to transform the current manual invoice payment processing. Your immediate task is to plan a requirement gathering workshop involving stakeholders Madhavi Pixel and Rene Zynga. Through this exercise, your job is to comprehend their requirements and establish the specifications for this new system.

1. Initial Step: What would you consider as your first step in this effort, and why?

2. Key Deliverables: What types of artifacts or documentation would you intend to deliver for this effort?

3. Framing Use-Cases: Can you think of two potential use-cases for this automated invoice processing system? Also draw a use-case diagram for them.

4. Constructing User Stories: How would you frame two examples of user stories related to this system?

5. Anticipating Reporting Requirements: Can you predict two types of reporting requirements that Madhavi and Rene might need from this system?

6. Dialogue with Stakeholders: What are three critical questions you would pose to Madhavi and Rene to understand their needs better?

7. Maintaining Professional Boundaries: Is there anything you would avoid asking Madhavi and Rene during these workshops?

8. Business Requirements Document (BRD): How would you go about creating a Business Requirements Document (BRD) for the Automated Invoice System?

9. Business Case: Considering the objective of transitioning from manual to automated invoice processing, construct a high-level business case for this project. What are the potential benefits and cost implications? How does this initiative align with the organization's broader strategic objectives? Additionally, what potential risks and mitigation strategies can you identify?

In this case study, you'll be applying fundamental concepts of business analysis, such as requirements elicitation, stakeholder management, and use-case development. Your approach might involve methodologies like Agile for iterative development and continuous feedback incorporation. As the Business Analyst, your role is to serve as the intermediary between business needs (as presented by Madhavi and Rene) and the technical team responsible for developing the automated system.

Case Study 7: Solutions

Solution 1: Initial Step

The initial step in this scenario would involve a thorough review of the project's scope, objectives, and requirements as defined by the Project Manager, Peter Slack. Following this, an examination of the existing manual paperwork process for invoice submission and payment processing is crucial. This research enables an understanding of the current process, highlights pain points, and uncovers potential areas of improvement. Identification of the key stakeholders, their roles, responsibilities, and their specific needs and requirements forms an integral part of this phase. The concluding part of this step entails the formulation of a comprehensive plan for the requirements gathering workshop. This includes establishing the agenda, assembling necessary materials, and planning the logistics.

Solution 2: Key Deliverables

As a Business Analyst, you would deliver various artifacts/documentation for this effort, including:

Business requirements document (BRD): This document outlines the high-level business requirements for the automated system that converts manual paperwork into a digital format for invoice submission and payment processing.

Functional requirements document (FRD): This document provides detailed specifications for the features and functionalities of the automated system, including the inputs, outputs, and processes involved.

Use cases: These are detailed scenarios that describe how users will interact with the automated system and achieve their goals.

Process flows: These are visual representations of the processes involved in the automated system, showing how information flows between different system components and users.

Test cases: These are documented procedures to verify that the system meets the requirements and works as intended.

User manuals: These are documentation that helps users understand how to use the system, including the interface and features.

Change management plan: This plan outlines how changes to the system will be managed and communicated to stakeholders.

The type of documentation and artifacts delivered may vary based on the project's scope, stakeholders' needs, and the project's development methodology.

Solution 3: Framing Use-Cases

Below are two examples of use cases for the automated system that converts manual paperwork into a digital format for invoice submission and payment processing:

Submitting an invoice for payment:

The user logs in to the system, navigates to the "Submit Invoice" function, and uploads the necessary documentation, including a copy of the invoice and any supporting documents. The system then validates the information and confirms that it meets the business and functional requirements. If there are any issues, the system generates an error message to notify the user. Once validated, the system saves the invoice and supporting documents in the appropriate location and generates an email notification to the relevant approver(s).

Reviewing an invoice for payment:

The user logs in to the system, navigates to the "Review Invoice" function, and views the list of pending invoices awaiting approval. The user selects an invoice for review and views the associated documentation, including the invoice and supporting documents. The user then validates the information and confirms that it meets the business and functional requirements. If there are any issues, the user can reject the invoice and provide comments for the submitter. If approved, the system saves the invoice and supporting documents in the appropriate location and generates an email notification to the relevant accounting team(s) for payment processing.

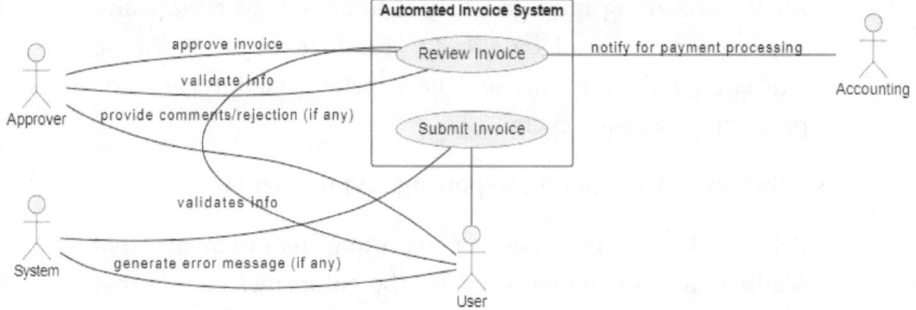

The above use case diagram shows how User interacts with "Submit Invoice" and "Review Invoice" use cases.

The "Submit Invoice" use case interacts with the System to validate the information. If there are any errors, the System will send an error message to the User.

The "Review Invoice" use case interacts with the Approver to validate the information. If there are any issues, the Approver can provide comments or rejection to the User. If the invoice is approved, it interacts with the Accounting department for payment processing.

Solution 4: Constructing User Stories

Below are two examples of a user story for the automated system that converts manual paperwork into a digital format for invoice submission and payment processing:

As an accounts payable clerk, I want to be able to submit an invoice electronically, so that I can eliminate the need for manual paperwork and ensure timely payment processing.

151

As an accounting manager, I want to be able to review and approve invoices electronically, so that I can increase efficiency, reduce errors, and have better visibility into the payment processing cycle.

Solution 5: Anticipating Reporting Requirements

Below are two examples of reporting requirements that Madhavi and Rene may need for the automated system that converts manual paperwork into a digital format for invoice submission and payment processing:

Invoice Processing Metrics Report: This report should provide a summary of key performance indicators (KPIs) related to invoice processing, including the number of invoices received, the number of invoices processed, the average processing time, and the percentage of invoices processed within a specified timeframe. This report would help Madhavi and Rene monitor the efficiency and effectiveness of the automated system and identify any areas for improvement.

Invoice Payment Status Report: This report should provide a real-time view of the status of payments for all submitted invoices, including those that are pending, approved, and paid. The report should also provide a breakdown of the payment status by vendor, invoice type, and payment method. This report would help Madhavi and Rene monitor the payment cycle and ensure timely payments to vendors.

Solution 6: Dialogue with Stakeholders

Below are three questions a Business Analyst could ask Madhavi and Rene before the requirements gathering workshop:

- What are the current pain points and challenges in the manual paperwork process for invoice submission and payment processing, and how are they impacting the business?
- What are the critical success factors for the automated system that will ensure its acceptance and adoption by the stakeholders, and how can we measure and monitor these factors?
- What are the risks and potential roadblocks that could impact the success of this project, and how can we mitigate these risks and overcome these roadblocks?

Solution 7: Maintaining Professional Boundaries

There are some things that a Business Analyst should avoid asking Madhavi and Rene during the workshop, such as:

- Avoid asking questions that are too technical or specific to the underlying technology stack unless Madhavi and Rene have expertise in this area.
- Avoid asking leading or biased questions that may influence or sway the responses of Madhavi and Rene. It is important to remain neutral and objective during the workshop.
- Avoid asking questions that are irrelevant or tangential to the project requirements, as this can waste time and distract from the main objectives of the workshop.

- Avoid making assumptions about the current process or system without first seeking clarification and validation from Madhavi and Rene. It is important to gather accurate and complete information before making any recommendations or proposals.

Solution 8: Business Requirements Document (BRD)

Crafting a Business Requirements Document (BRD) for an Automated Invoice System requires a deep understanding of the current system and the needs that the automation should address. This document should highlight the business rationale behind the project, specifying the project's objectives, scope, and functional and non-functional requirements. Below is a high-level approach a Business Analyst might take:

1. **Project Background:** The first section of the BRD should detail the reasons for the project and the problems that the proposed solution is expected to solve. In this case, the issues would likely relate to inefficiencies and errors in the existing manual invoice processing system.

2. **Business Objectives and Success Criteria:** This section should outline the overall objectives of implementing the Automated Invoice System, as well as how success will be measured. For instance, objectives might include reducing errors, increasing speed, and improving tracking of invoices.

3. **Project Scope:** The project's scope should be outlined, detailing what is included and what is not. The scope might encompass migrating all existing invoices to the

new system, integrating the system with existing financial software, and training staff to use the system.

4. **Functional Requirements:** These are the actions that the system must be able to perform. For the Automated Invoice System, functional requirements might include the ability to create invoices, send reminders for unpaid invoices, and generate reports.

5. **Non-Functional Requirements:** This covers criteria not related to specific behaviours, such as performance requirements, security, reliability, and compatibility with existing systems.

6. **User Requirements:** This section outlines what different types of users should be able to do within the system. There may be different types of users, such as finance staff and managers, each with their unique needs.

7. **Constraints and Assumptions:** Any constraints (budget, time, technology) and assumptions made during the planning process should be listed out. For example, the project might assume that all staff have basic computer literacy skills.

8. **Acceptance Criteria:** Define what must be true for the project to be accepted by the stakeholders. These criteria should be SMART (Specific, Measurable, Achievable, Relevant, Time-Bound).

Once the BRD is created, it should be reviewed and approved by key stakeholders before moving forward with development. It serves as a guiding document for the technical team and provides a reference point against which the final solution can be validated.

A sample Business Requirements Document (BRD) for the Automated Invoice System might look like below:

Business Requirement Document for Automated Invoice Processing System

Introduction

Purpose and scope of the document

The purpose of this Business Requirement Document is to define the requirements for the development of an automated invoice processing system. This document is intended for use by the development team and stakeholders involved in the project.

The scope of this document includes the functional and non-functional requirements for the system, as well as any assumptions and constraints. The functional requirements describe the system's capabilities, such as the ability to capture and process invoices, while the non-functional requirements describe the system's performance, security, and usability characteristics.

The system will be developed using Agile methodology, with iterative development and testing. The system must comply with all applicable laws and regulations related to invoice processing and payment.

The stakeholders involved in this project include the project sponsor, the project manager, the business analyst, the development team, and the end-users who will be using the system to submit and approve invoices.

The goal of the system is to automate the invoice processing workflow and improve efficiency and accuracy. The system should be intuitive and user-friendly, with minimal training required for end-users.

Business context and background information

The current invoice processing system is entirely manual, resulting in inefficiencies and delays in processing invoices for payment. The manual system involves a paper-based process, where invoices are printed and mailed to the accounts payable department. The invoices are then manually reviewed, approved, and entered into the accounting system for payment processing. This process is time-consuming and error-prone, leading to delays in payments to vendors and suppliers.

The organization's growth has resulted in a significant increase in the number of invoices processed, leading to a backlog of invoices waiting to be processed. This backlog has resulted in delayed payments to vendors and suppliers, negatively impacting the organization's relationships with its business partners.

The organization has identified the need for an automated invoice processing system to improve the efficiency and accuracy of the invoice processing workflow. The automated system will replace the manual process, reducing the time and effort required to process invoices. The system will also improve the accuracy of invoice processing, reducing errors and ensuring timely payments to vendors and suppliers.

The organization has allocated a budget of $500,000 for the development and implementation of the automated invoice processing system. The project is expected to take six months to complete, with the system going live at the end of the development cycle. The system will be developed using Agile methodology, with iterative development and testing to ensure that the system meets the requirements of the organization and its stakeholders.

Business goals and objectives

The goal of the automated invoice processing system is to improve the efficiency and accuracy of the invoice processing workflow. The objectives of the system are:

OBJ 1: Reduce the time required to process invoices: The system should automate the invoice processing workflow, reducing the time required to process invoices from receipt to payment.

OBJ 2: Improve the accuracy of invoice processing: The system should reduce errors in the processing of invoices, resulting in more accurate and timely payments to vendors and suppliers.

OBJ 3: Improve visibility and control: The system should provide greater visibility and control over the invoice processing workflow, allowing the organization to track the status of invoices and payments and identify bottlenecks and issues.

OBJ 4: Enhance communication and collaboration: The system should enhance communication and collaboration between the accounts payable department and the vendors and suppliers, improving the organization's relationships with its business partners.

OBJ 5: Reduce paper-based processes: The system should reduce the organization's dependence on paper-based processes, resulting in a more sustainable and environmentally friendly approach to invoice processing.

The success of the automated invoice processing system will be measured by the following key performance indicators:

KPI 1: Reduction in the time required to process invoices.

KPI 2: Reduction in the number of errors in the processing of invoices.

KPI 3: Increase in the percentage of invoices processed electronically.

KPI 4: Improvement in vendor and supplier satisfaction.

KPI 5: Reduction in the overall cost of invoice processing.

Stakeholder Analysis

Identification of key stakeholders and their roles in the project

The success of the automated invoice processing system will depend on the involvement and support of a range of stakeholders across the organization. The following stakeholders have been identified as key to the success of the project:

Accounts Payable Department: The accounts payable department is responsible for processing invoices and making payments to vendors and suppliers. They will be the primary users of the automated invoice processing system and will be responsible for ensuring that the system is used effectively and efficiently.

IT Department: The IT department will be responsible for implementing the automated invoice processing system and ensuring that it integrates effectively with existing systems and infrastructure. They will also be responsible for providing technical support to users of the system.

Finance Department: The finance department is responsible for managing the organization's financial resources and ensuring that invoices are processed accurately and timely. They will be responsible for monitoring the performance of the automated invoice processing system and ensuring that it meets the organization's financial reporting requirements.

Vendors and Suppliers: Vendors and suppliers will be required to submit invoices electronically through the automated invoice processing system. They will also be able to track the status of their invoices and payments through the system.

Management: Senior management will be responsible for providing the strategic direction and support for the project. They will also be responsible for ensuring that the project is aligned with the organization's goals and objectives.

End-users: The end-users of the system are the individuals who will be directly interacting with the system. They will be responsible for submitting and approving invoices through the system.

The following table outlines the roles and responsibilities of the key stakeholders:

Stakeholder	Role	Responsibilities
Accounts Payable Department	User	Primary users of the system; responsible for ensuring the system is used effectively and efficiently
IT Department	Implementer	Responsible for implementing the system and providing technical support
Finance Department	Monitor	Responsible for monitoring the performance of the system and ensuring it meets financial reporting requirements
Vendors and Suppliers	User	Required to submit invoices electronically and can track status of invoices and payments
Management	Sponsor	Provides strategic direction and support for the project
End-users	User	Responsible for submitting and approving invoices through the system

Assessment of stakeholder needs and expectations.

The success of the automated invoice processing system will depend on meeting the needs and expectations of the key stakeholders involved in the project. A comprehensive assessment of stakeholder needs and expectations has been conducted, and the following requirements have been identified:

Accounts Payable Department: The accounts payable department requires a system that is easy to use and can process invoices accurately and quickly. The system must also be able to integrate with existing accounting systems and provide real-time visibility into the status of invoices and payments.

IT Department: The IT department requires a system that is secure, scalable, and can be integrated with existing systems and infrastructure. The system must also be easy to maintain and provide robust reporting capabilities.

Finance Department: The finance department requires a system that can streamline the invoice processing workflow and reduce errors and discrepancies. The system must also provide real-time visibility into the status of invoices and payments and enable accurate and timely financial reporting.

Vendors and Suppliers: Vendors and suppliers require a system that is easy to use and can enable them to submit invoices electronically. The system must also provide real-time visibility into the status of invoices and payments and enable them to track the progress of their invoices.

Management: Senior management requires a system that can provide real-time visibility into the financial performance of the organization. The system must also be able to support strategic decision-making by providing accurate and timely financial data.

End-users: End-users require a system that is easy to use and can enable them to submit and approve invoices quickly and accurately. The system must also provide real-time visibility into the status of invoices and payments and enable them to track the progress of their invoices.

Based on the assessment of stakeholder needs and expectations, the following requirements have been identified for the automated invoice processing system:

The system must be easy to use and able to process invoices accurately and quickly.

The system must be secure, scalable, and able to integrate with existing systems and infrastructure.

The system must provide real-time visibility into the status of invoices and payments.

The system must enable accurate and timely financial reporting.

The system must be able to streamline the invoice processing workflow and reduce errors and discrepancies.

The system must provide robust reporting capabilities.

The system must enable vendors and suppliers to submit invoices electronically and track the progress of their invoices.

The system must provide real-time visibility into the financial performance of the organization.

The system must enable end-users to submit and approve invoices quickly and accurately.

Analysis of stakeholder influence and involvement in the project

It is important to identify the level of influence and involvement of each stakeholder in the project to understand their expectations, requirements, and constraints. This analysis will help us to prioritize their needs and ensure their engagement throughout the project.

The following table summarizes the key stakeholders, their level of influence, and their expected involvement in the project:

Stakeholder	Level of Influence	Expected Involvement
Peter Slack, Project Manager	High	Project Sponsor and Leader
Madhavi Pixel, Accounts Manager	High	Subject Matter Expert (SME), End-user, Decision Maker
Rene Zynga, IT Manager	High	SME, End-user, Decision Maker
Accounts Payable Team	Medium	End-users, SME
IT Development Team	Medium	Developers, Technical SME

Finance Department	Low	Stakeholder, Provider	Information
HR Department	Low	Stakeholder, Provider	Information

Peter Slack, Madhavi Pixel, and Rene Zynga have high levels of influence in the project as they are key decision-makers and stakeholders. The Accounts Payable and IT Development teams will be involved in the project as end-users and SMEs. The Finance and HR departments are stakeholders who will provide information and support as needed.

The analysis of stakeholder influence and involvement will be used to prioritize stakeholder needs and ensure that they are engaged throughout the project. Regular communication and stakeholder updates will be provided to maintain their involvement and support.

Functional Requirements

Ref No.	Requirement Title	Requirement Description	MoSCoW Priority
HL_FR001	User Authentication and Authorization	The system shall allow user authentication and authorization.	
FR1.1	Account Creation	The system shall allow users to create and manage their own accounts.	Must

Ref No.	Requirement Title	Requirement Description	MoSCoW Priority
FR1.2	Multi-Factor Authentication	The system shall provide two-factor authentication for added security.	Should
FR1.3	Roles Based Access	The system shall restrict access to features and data based on user roles and permissions.	Must
HL_FR002	Invoice Management	The system shall allow Invoice Management	
FR2.1	Invoice Storage	The system shall allow users to upload and store invoices.	Must
FR2.2	Invoice Data	The system shall extract relevant data from the invoices and populate the system's database.	Must
FR2.3	Invoice Editing	The system shall allow users to view and edit invoices.	Must
FR2.4	Automated Workflow	The system shall provide an automated workflow to approve or reject invoices.	Should
FR2.5	Notifications	The system shall generate notifications to inform users of the status of their invoices.	Could
HL_FR003	Payment Processing	The system shall allow Payment processing.	
FR3.1	Integration	The system shall	Must

Ref No.	Requirement Title	Requirement Description	MoSCoW Priority
		integrate with the company's existing payment gateway.	
FR3.2	Payment	The system shall allow users to initiate payment requests for approved invoices.	Must
FR3.3	Status	The system shall allow users to view payment status and history.	Must
HL_FR004	Reporting and Analytics	The system shall provide Reporting and Analytics.	
FR4.1	Reporting	The system shall provide real-time reporting on invoice status and payment history.	Won't
FR4.2	Custom Reports	The system shall allow users to generate custom reports based on various criteria.	Should
FR4.3	Analytics	The system shall provide analytics and insights on payment processing performance.	Must
HL_FR005	System Administration	The System shall allow system administration.	
FR5.1	Console Management	The system shall provide an	Must

Ref No.	Requirement Title	Requirement Description	MoSCoW Priority
		administrative console to manage user accounts and roles.	
FR5.2	Database Tools	The system shall provide tools to manage the system's database, including backups and restores.	Could
FR5.3	Audit	The system shall provide an audit trail of user actions and system events.	Must

Non-Functional Requirements

The below non-functional requirements will ensure that the Automated Invoice Processing System is reliable, secure, scalable, and user-friendly. By meeting these requirements, the system will be able to support the business in processing invoices and payments efficiently and effectively.

Ref No.	Requirement Title	Requirement Description	MoSCoW Priority
NFR001	Usability	The system should be user-friendly and easy to navigate for all authorized users. The system should also provide clear and concise instructions for all tasks and functions.	Must

Ref No.	Requirement Title	Requirement Description	MoSCoW Priority
NFR002	Reliability	The system should be available 24/7, with minimal downtime for maintenance or upgrades. The system should also be able to recover from any failures or errors without losing data or corrupting the system.	Must
NFR003	Security	The system should ensure that all data is protected from unauthorized access or modification. The system should also comply with relevant security standards and regulations.	Should
NFR004	Scalability	The system should be able to handle an increasing volume of invoices and payments as the business grows. The system should also be able to support additional users and functionality without impacting performance.	Must
NFR005	Compatibility	The system should be compatible with existing business applications and systems, including accounting and financial software.	Must

Ref No.	Requirement Title	Requirement Description	MoSCoW Priority
NFR006	Performance	The system should be able to process invoices and payments within a reasonable timeframe, even during peak usage periods. The system should also be able to handle a high volume of transactions without compromising performance.	Should

Reporting Requirements

The below reporting requirements will provide stakeholders with real-time information on the status of invoices and payments, as well as the ability to audit and track invoice processing activities. These reports will help stakeholders make informed business decisions and identify areas for process improvement.

Ref No.	Requirement Title	Requirement Description	Frequency
RR001	Key Performance Indicators	The system shall generate reports on invoice processing metrics, such as processing time, error rates, and payment status.	Ad-Hoc
RR002	Dashboards and	The system shall	Real-Time

Ref No.	Requirement Title	Requirement Description	Frequency
	Alerts	provide real-time dashboards and alerts for key performance indicators (KPIs) related to invoice processing.	
RR003	Invoice Status Report	This report should provide a summary of all invoices processed by the system, including their current status (e.g., approved, pending, rejected), the date of submission, and the amount invoiced. This report should be available to authorized users on a weekly basis.	Weekly
RR004	Payment Processing Report	This report should provide a summary of all payments processed by the system, including the payment amount, the date of payment, and the payment status (e.g., completed, pending). This report should be available to authorized users on a	Monthly

Ref No.	Requirement Title	Requirement Description	Frequency
		monthly basis.	
RR005	Audit Trail Report	This report should provide a detailed history of all actions taken on a particular invoice, including the date and time of each action, the user who performed the action, and the result of the action (e.g., approved, rejected). This report should be available to authorized users upon request.	Ad-Hoc
RR006	Exception Report	This report should identify any invoices that were not processed by the system due to errors or exceptions (e.g., missing data, incorrect information). This report should be available to authorized users on a daily basis.	Daily

Assumptions and Constraints

Assumptions:

172

AS01: The stakeholders Madhavi Pixel and Rene Zynga will be available and actively participate in the requirement gathering workshops.

AS02: The Automated Invoice Processing System will be integrated with the existing enterprise resource planning (ERP) system.

AS03: Sufficient budget and resources will be allocated to the project to support the development and implementation of the Automated Invoice Processing System.

AS04: The end-users will have the necessary skills and knowledge to use the Automated Invoice Processing System effectively.

AS05: The system will be developed using Agile methodology with iterative development and testing.

Constraints:

CS01: The project must be completed within a six-month timeframe.

CS02: The Automated Invoice Processing System must comply with all relevant legal and regulatory requirements.

CS03: The development and implementation of the Automated Invoice Processing System must not disrupt existing business operations.

CS04: The Automated Invoice Processing System must be compatible with the existing hardware and software infrastructure.

Glossary of Terms

This glossary of terms will provide a shared understanding of key terms and concepts used in the document and throughout the project. It will help to ensure that all stakeholders have a common language and reduce any confusion or misunderstandings that may arise.

Accounts Payable: A department within an organization that manages and processes invoices from vendors and suppliers for payment.

Automated Invoice Processing System: A software application that automates the processing of invoices for payment, eliminating the need for manual paperwork.

Business Analyst: A professional who works with stakeholders to elicit, analyze, and document business requirements.

End-user: A person or system that will use the Automated Invoice Processing System to perform tasks and functions.

Invoice: A document sent by a vendor or supplier to request payment for goods or services.

Project Manager: A professional responsible for planning, executing, and closing projects, and managing project teams.

Stakeholder: An individual, group, or organization that has an interest in the project or can be affected by its outcome.

Subject Matter Expert (SME): A person who has specialized knowledge and expertise in a particular area relevant to the project.

User Story: A brief narrative that describes a feature or requirement from an end-user's perspective.

Use Case: A description of the interactions between a user and the Automated Invoice Processing System to achieve a specific goal.

Distribution List and Document Approval

Date	Approver	Role	Version	Note if sign off required	Evidence of Approval
06.05.2023	Peter Slack	Project Manager	1.0	Review and Sign Off	Approval Email
10.05.2023	Madhavi Pixel	Accounts Manager	1.1	Review and Sign Off	Approval Email
16.05.2023	Rene Zynga	IT Manager	1.1	Review and Sign Off	Approval Email

Solution 9: Business Case

When constructing a business case for the transition from manual to automated invoice processing, a business analyst should consider a range of factors:

Benefits:

1. **Efficiency:** Automation could significantly reduce the time taken to process invoices, thereby freeing up resources for other tasks.

2. **Accuracy:** Automated systems could help minimize human errors that occur during manual processing.

3. **Cost savings:** Over time, the cost savings from reduced labor and increased efficiency could outweigh the initial costs of implementing the new system.

4. **Transparency and auditability:** Automated systems can offer improved tracking of invoice processing, making it easier to audit and monitor the process.

Cost Implications:

1. **Initial setup and implementation costs:** This includes the costs of purchasing and setting up the new system, as well as any costs associated with migrating data from the old system.

2. **Training costs:** Staff members will need to be trained to use the new system.

3. **Maintenance costs:** Ongoing costs to maintain, upgrade and troubleshoot the system should also be considered.

Alignment with strategic objectives: An automated invoice system could align with broader strategic goals such as digital transformation, operational efficiency, cost reduction, or enhanced customer service (e.g., faster invoice processing leading to quicker service delivery).

Potential Risks and Mitigation Strategies:

1. **Resistance to change:** This can be mitigated by effective change management, including communication, training, and support.

2. **Implementation delays or cost overruns:** These can be managed by employing robust project management practices, and by selecting reliable technology vendors.

3. **Data migration issues or loss:** A comprehensive data migration and backup plan can help address this risk.

4. **System glitches or failures:** Regular maintenance and having a robust contingency plan can help mitigate this risk.

In summary, a business case should present a compelling argument, based on clear evidence, that the benefits of implementing the automated invoice system outweigh the costs, risks, and change management efforts. It should also show how this initiative aligns with the organization's strategic objectives.

A sample Business Case for the Automated Invoice System might look like below:

Business Case for Automated Invoice Processing System

1. Executive Summary:

This business case outlines the reasons for implementing an Automated Invoice Processing System, replacing the existing manual paperwork process. The key objective is to increase efficiency, reduce errors, and achieve cost savings over time.

2. The Business Problem:

The current manual invoice processing system is time-consuming and prone to errors. It also lacks the necessary transparency and is not easily auditable. There is a need to improve this process, to ensure faster and more accurate invoice processing.

3. Proposed Solution:

The proposed solution is an Automated Invoice Processing System. This system will automate the invoicing process, reducing human errors, enhancing speed and increasing the overall efficiency of the system.

4. Benefits:

- **Efficiency**: The new system will significantly cut down the time required for invoice processing.

- **Accuracy**: The automated system will minimize human errors, ensuring more accuracy.

- **Cost Savings**: The efficiency and accuracy of the new system will lead to substantial cost savings in the long run.

- **Transparency and Auditability**: The new system will provide better transparency and will be easily auditable.

5. Costs:

- **Initial Implementation Costs**: The upfront cost of acquiring and setting up the system.

- **Training Costs**: Costs associated with training the staff on the new system.

- **Maintenance Costs**: Ongoing costs to maintain and upgrade the system.

6. Strategic Alignment:

The implementation of the Automated Invoice Processing System aligns with the company's strategic goals of digital transformation, operational efficiency, and cost reduction.

7. Risks and Mitigation Strategies:

- **Resistance to Change**: This will be managed through a well-planned change management strategy, involving communication, training, and support.

- **Implementation Delays and Cost Overruns**: Robust project management practices will be used to manage these risks.

- **Data Migration Issues or Loss**: A comprehensive data migration and backup plan will be put in place to mitigate this risk.

- **System Glitches or Failures**: Regular maintenance and a robust contingency plan will be used to manage this risk.

8. Conclusion:

The implementation of an Automated Invoice Processing System presents a valuable opportunity for the organization to improve efficiency, reduce costs, and minimize errors. The investment is justifiable given the substantial benefits and alignment with strategic objectives.

Cracking the Business Analyst Interview

Transitioning into the role of a Business Analyst can be a rewarding move for individuals from varied professional backgrounds. This career path not only requires a deep understanding of business analysis concepts but also entails the development of key interpersonal skills and the ability to effectively demonstrate these competencies during interviews. This chapter has been crafted to guide you on this journey, arming you with the necessary tools and insights that will pave the way for a fruitful career in Business Analysis.

This chapter unfolds across several sections, each designed to equip you with indispensable tools and strategies:

1. **Resume Preparation**: This section guides you on how to create compelling resumes that effectively spotlight your unique skills and experiences. Sample resumes for both a seasoned Senior Business Analyst and an aspiring Graduate Business Analyst will be provided as templates to help you craft your own.

2. **Transitioning from Different Backgrounds**: A dedicated section for professionals aspiring to transition into Business Analysis from diverse professional

backgrounds. It will provide insights into how to leverage existing skills, acquire new ones, and how to position oneself in the BA job market.

3. **Further Learning and Certifications**: Here, we explore various online platforms offering free and paid courses to enhance your knowledge and understanding of the BA field. The importance of professional certifications and their role in boosting your credibility will also be discussed.

4. **Understanding Interview Questions**: This section delves into the types of questions asked during a Business Analyst interview. From technical and behavioural questions to case study problems, you'll gain insights into what employers seek and how best to prepare your responses.

5. **Real-Life Interview Insights with Sample Answers**: This comprehensive section offers a deep dive into actual Business Analyst interviews, complete with authentic questions and exemplary answers. It's designed to equip you with a robust understanding of the typical job description and helps you craft compelling, personalized responses. Additionally, it provides invaluable tips and strategies to successfully navigate the entire interview process, from initial preparation to concluding with confidence. By examining real-world scenarios and expert guidance, you'll gain the insights needed to excel in your Business Analyst interviews and make a lasting impression on potential employers.

6. **Job Search Tips**: Finding your ideal Business Analyst role requires more than sifting through countless job postings; it requires strategic thinking and diligence. This final section guides you through key strategies, such as recognizing and exploring allied roles that might suit your skills, focusing on top job portals in your country, proactively building rapport with recruiters, and maintaining persistence and patience in your search. With these tactics, you'll be well on your way to securing a position that aligns with your career path and ambitions.

This chapter will take you on a journey with two distinct candidates: the experienced Senior Business Analyst and the eager Graduate Business Analyst. Learn from their experiences, prepare yourself for your career transition, and gain practical insights to ace your Business Analyst interviews.

No matter your professional background, transitioning into a Business Analyst role is achievable with the right knowledge, skills, and guidance. We hope this chapter empowers you to crack the Business Analyst interview and thrive in your desired role.

Business Analyst Resume Preparation

Crafting an effective resume is akin to creating a compelling narrative that highlights your professional growth, skills development, and achievements, painting a vivid picture of your capabilities. The key to a successful business analyst resume lies not only in showcasing relevant skills, experiences, certifications, and accomplishments but also in the strategic use of keywords that align with the role you're applying for.

If you are a seasoned Senior Business Analyst, your resume should demonstrate your leadership, project management experiences, and specific industry expertise. Detailing complex projects you've managed, including key challenges, solutions implemented, and results achieved, can be impactful. Incorporate relevant keywords and terminologies such as Agile, Scrum, or BPMN. These not only underscore your professional worth but also enhance your appeal to potential employers by aligning with their likely search criteria.

For aspiring Graduate/Entry Level Business Analysts lacking extensive professional experiences, don't despair. Focus on relevant coursework, internships, capstone projects, or academic experiences that have allowed you to develop business analysis skills. Emphasize your abilities in problem-solving, communication, and team collaboration, using specific keywords related to these soft skills that are highly valued in the Business Analyst role. Such careful keyword inclusion will help your resume stand out to recruiters.

Now, let's consider how you can articulate your transferable skills from non-BA roles. For instance, if you worked as a Sales Associate, a typical bullet point might read, "Maintained knowledge of products to effectively sell to customers." To make this more relevant to a Business Analyst role, you could rephrase it as, "Leveraged product knowledge to identify customer needs, analyze purchasing trends, and suggest sales strategies - a process similar to the requirement elicitation and stakeholder analysis in business analysis." Similarly, if you were a Project Assistant, a bullet point might be, "Assisted in coordinating project activities and managing timelines." This could be reworded as, "Managed project schedules and coordinated tasks, demonstrating organization and coordination skills similar to a business analyst's role in project management." By rewording your experiences in this way, you can illustrate to recruiters how the skills you've gained in non-BA roles are transferrable and valuable to a Business Analyst position.

The purpose of your resume is to spark interest and secure an interview. Every section, be it the summary, professional experience, education, certifications, or skills, should align with the needs of the role you're applying for and be enriched with relevant keywords that resonate with the job description.

To assist your resume-building process, sample resumes for both the Senior Business Analyst and the Graduate Business Analyst are provided in the following sections. Use these templates as inspiration, taking cues from their effective structure, content, and keyword utilization.

Mastering the art of resume writing, including the strategic use of industry-specific keywords, is a vital step towards securing your dream Business Analyst role. Use this section as a comprehensive guide to create a stellar resume that authentically represents you and resonates with recruiters and applicant tracking systems.

Below is a comma-separated list of common keywords that might be relevant for a Business Analyst resume: Requirements Gathering, Data Analysis, Process Improvement, Stakeholder Management, Agile Methodology, Scrum, SWOT Analysis, Project Management, SQL, Risk Assessment, Business Intelligence, Change Management, Use Case, Workflow Analysis, KPIs, Metrics, Lean Six Sigma, Gap Analysis, Business Strategy, User Stories, Prototyping, ERP, SAP, CRM, Tableau, Financial Analysis, Strategic Planning, Team Collaboration, Quality Assurance, UAT (User Acceptance Testing), Feasibility Studies, Compliance, Reporting Tools, Cross-functional Team Leadership, Problem-solving, Decision-making, Cost-benefit Analysis, Vendor Management, Communication Skills, Time Management, Collaboration Tools, JIRA, Excel, PMP (Project Management Professional), Data Visualization, Business Process Modelling, Systems Analysis, Root Cause Analysis, Market Research, Innovation Management, SDLC (Software Development Life Cycle), ITIL (Information Technology Infrastructure Library).

Sample Senior Business Analyst Resume

Richard Baker

London | 0770000710 | RichardBaker@hotmail.co.uk

Summary

Highly skilled and detail-oriented business analyst with 5 years of experience in analyzing and improving business processes. Seeking a challenging position where I can leverage my analytical skills, problem-solving abilities, and strong business acumen to drive organizational growth and success. Polished in formulating business improvement strategies and overseeing new technology and system implementation. Commercially aware professional with in-depth knowledge of computing systems and project management techniques.

Education

Bachelor's degree: Economics

Amazing University   Turkey

Skills

- Business process analysis and improvement

- Requirement gathering and documentation.

- Data analysis and interpretation

- Process mapping and optimization

- Agile methodologies

- Strong analytical and problem-solving skills

- Excellent written and

- Stakeholder management
- Project management
- Business case development

- verbal communication
- Forecasting and Planning
- Competitive Market Analysis

Experience

Business Analyst   **10/2021 to 04/2023**

V Group Inc.   **London**

- Implementation of a payment management portal for facilitating end-user payments for a law firm

- Conducted thorough analysis of business processes, identified areas for improvement, and developed recommendations to enhance operational efficiency.

- Collaborated with cross-functional teams to gather requirements, elicited stakeholder feedback, and ensured alignment with business goals and objectives.

- Created detailed requirement documents, use cases, and functional specifications to facilitate development and implementation of new payment system Self Pay

- Create Epics and User stories and help drive the agile development process forward via SCRUM ceremonies.

- Acted as liaison between business stakeholders and Offshore IT teams to translate business requirements into technical specifications.

Business Analyst   **07/2020 to 08/2021**

Motivity Labs Inc   **Remote/London**

- Worked on automated financing model based on technology-driven business processes for a consumer finance company.

- Assisted senior business analysts in gathering requirements and conducting gap analysis for process improvement initiatives.

- Developed and maintained project documentation, including business process maps, requirements traceability matrices, and user manuals.

- Translate business concerns into clear requirements through use cases, process diagrams, business and/or functional requirements so they are understandable and usable by each stakeholder group.

- Participate in Agile SCRUM meetings to facilitate mapping user stories to process solutions and providing guidance on release schedules that are effective and efficient for the end-user.

- Supported user acceptance testing by creating test scenarios, executing test cases, and documenting results.

- Managed projects and served as primary liaison between client and multiple internal groups to clarify goals and meet standards and deadlines.

Business Analyst   01/2018 to 01/2020

CyanGate, LLC   **Turkey**

- Improvement of retail workflows by enabling a Product Information Management (PIM) system for Auto-Tagging.

- Acted as a liaison between business stakeholders and IT teams to translate business requirements into technical specifications.

- Led and participated in Agile project teams, actively contributing to sprint planning, backlog grooming, and sprint reviews.

- Collaborated with end-users to conduct user acceptance testing, ensuring that systems and applications met defined business requirements.

- Prepared and delivered presentations to senior management, conveying complex information in a clear and concise manner.

- Monitored project progress, identified risks and issues, and proposed mitigation strategies to ensure timely delivery and successful outcomes.

Accomplishments

189

- Implemented a process automation initiative that resulted in 20% reduction in execution time and increased overall customer satisfaction.

- Led cross-functional team in the successful implementation of a new payment system, resulting in improved data accuracy and increased efficiency in customer relationship management.

References

- Available upon request

Sample Graduate Business Analyst Resume

Emily Thompson

Location: Manchester, UK | **(M)** +44 1234567890 | **(E)**
emily.thompson@example.com

SUMMARY

Diligent and goal-oriented professional with an educational background in Business & Management, and foundational knowledge in data analysis techniques, statistical modeling, and data visualization tools. Eager to contribute technical expertise to support data-driven decision-making processes. Emphasizes collaboration, a positive attitude, and robust communication skills.

IT SKILLS

- **SQL** (Big Query, MySQL & SQL Server) | Advance

- **Tableau & Power BI** | Intermediate

- **Microsoft Excel** (VLOOKUP, Pivot Tables, Conditional Formatting, Nested Functions) | Advance

PROFESSIONAL EXPERIENCE

Customer Service Manager | Entain Group London, UK | Mar 2021 – October 2022

- Analyzed and processed customer requests, resolving complaints to enhance consumer satisfaction through data-driven methods.

- Coordinated daily workflow procedures to improve shop ratings, leveraging data insights to guide team members' performance.

- Strategically expanded the customer base and boosted retention, achieving KPI metrics through the meticulous execution of loyalty programs.

- Utilized Power BI to track and measure performance, applying analytics to ensure success in meeting customer loyalty program targets.

Bar Manager | Chai Ki London, UK | Oct 2018 – Jun 2020

- Achieved high staff retention rates through the data-informed implementation of career development plans, training initiatives, and fostering a strong bar culture.

- Cultivated productive relationships with beverage companies, utilizing data analysis to drive successful collaborations and achieve mutually beneficial outcomes.

- Strengthened team collaboration through the introduction of inventive data-driven solutions, enhancing efficiency in task delegation and operations.

Bar Supervisor | Roka Restaurant London, UK | Feb 2016 – Oct 2018

- Managed and assigned bar duties to staff members, utilizing analytical tools to ensure seamless working functions.
- Organized regular staff training sessions, introducing newcomers to company standards through systematic data-driven methods.

EDUCATION

- **BA Business & Management** | University of Manchester, Manchester, UK | Sep 2020 – Jun 2023

- **Data Analytics Professional Certificate** | Coursera | May 2022 – Aug 2022

- **Diploma in Leadership & Management** | City College, London, UK | Sep 2019 – Jul 2020

- **HE Diploma in Business & Management** | Smithfield Community College, London, UK | May 2019 – Jul 2019

PROJECTS

- **Data Visualization Project** | Created a Global heatmap to visualize Covid-19 cases. (Tableau)

- **Exploratory Data Analysis Project** | Comparative market analysis of tech products. (SQL & Excel)

- **Research Project at University of Manchester** | Analyzed Quantitative & Qualitative data to study emerging business trends. (SPSS)

LANGUAGES

- **English** | Full Working Proficiency
- **French** | Intermediate Proficiency
- **German** | Basic Proficiency

Transitioning to Business Analyst Roles from Different Backgrounds

The business analysis field is marked by its versatility and adaptability. Regardless of your original profession, be it in customer service, marketing, IT, or otherwise, transitioning into a Business Analyst role can be an attainable and rewarding career move. The ubiquitous nature of BA skills means that with the right approach, relevant experience, certifications, and even entry-level enthusiasm, one can make this transition smoothly. This chapter delves into the necessary steps and insights to help guide this career change, using the example of an aspiring Graduate Business Analyst.

1. **Identify and Highlight Relevant BA Skills from Your Background**

A careful examination of your previous roles can unearth transferable skills that are highly valuable in a BA position. For example, Emily's role as a Customer Service Manager included responsibilities that demonstrate problem-solving, communication, and data analysis skills. Here's how you can derive BA skills from her experience:

- **Data Analysis Skills**: Use of Power BI to track and measure performance.

- **Problem-Solving**: Coordinated daily workflow procedures, improving shop rating standards.

- **Communication**: Fostered productive relationships with external vendors and managed internal teams.

2. Supplement Your Resume with Relevant BA Certifications

Enhance your BA profile by acquiring certifications related to the field. Emily obtained a Data Analytics Professional Certificate, emphasizing her dedication to technical expertise and continuous learning. Consider certificates from reputable platforms like Coursera, LinkedIn Learning, or IIBA that align with the BA domain.

3. Showcase Academic Background and Projects

If you are a recent graduate or have undertaken projects that reflect your BA capabilities, highlight them. Emily's BA in Business & Management and her Data Visualization and Exploratory Data Analysis projects exemplify her readiness to tackle real-world BA challenges.

4. Consider Entry-Level Roles or Leverage Industry Experience

For newcomers to the BA field, entry-level roles provide a gateway to build hands-on experience. Conversely, if your background aligns with a specific sector, you may apply directly to senior roles. Emily's hands-on experience with tools like SQL and Tableau, coupled with her management roles, could make her a candidate for both entry-level and specialized BA positions in the retail or hospitality sectors.

5. Soft Skills Matter

Don't overlook soft skills like collaboration, adaptability, and robust communication. These are essential in a BA role, as reflected in Emily's experience in team collaboration and customer satisfaction.

6. Language Proficiency

In a globalized world, knowing multiple languages can be an added advantage, as shown in Emily's proficiency in French and German.

Transitioning into a Business Analyst role is not confined by your professional background. With the right mix of showcasing relevant experience, adding certifications, targeting appropriate roles, and emphasizing both soft and hard skills, you can create a compelling case for your transition into this dynamic field. Emily's resume provides an inspiring template to guide you in crafting your own unique BA career path. The key is to identify and harness the BA skills inherent in your existing experiences and present them convincingly to potential employers. Whether you are a seasoned professional in a related field or an ambitious graduate, the BA world is open to diverse talents and backgrounds.

Free Business Analyst Certifications for your resume

In the rapidly evolving world of business, continuous learning is no longer a luxury but a necessity. It holds even more importance for a Business Analyst, given the diverse and dynamic nature of their role. The good news? You can find numerous online platforms that provide free and paid courses to help you continually enhance your BA skills and stay abreast of industry trends.

One such invaluable resource is LinkedIn Learning, a platform that offers a multitude of courses covering different aspects of business analysis, project management, Agile methodologies, and many more. As a new user, you can access a one-month free trial and leverage this period to complete several foundational courses such as:

- Business Analysis Foundations

- Agile Foundations

- How to Perform Business Analysis in a Virtual Environment

- Agile Project Management Foundations

- Project Management Foundations

- Learning Data Analytics

Upon completion of the courses, you'll receive a certificate from LinkedIn Learning that can be added to both your resume and LinkedIn profile, adding credibility and showcasing your continuous professional development.

Make the most of your one-month trial by enrolling in multiple courses, and delve into a variety of areas that pique your interest or complement your career path. It's a window of opportunity to bolster your professional toolbox and learn from industry experts without spending a dime.

Additionally, platforms like Coursera and edX offer a wide array of courses in business analysis and related fields. While most courses are paid, they occasionally offer free access to their course content, allowing you to gain knowledge without the certification.

For more formal certifications, consider globally recognized institutions such as the International Institute of Business Analysis (IIBA), the Project Management Institute (PMI), and the British Computer Society (BCS). These institutions provide globally recognized certifications such as Certification of Capability in Business Analysis (CCBA), Certified Business Analysis Professional (CBAP), PMI Professional in Business Analysis (PMI-PBA), and BCS International Diploma in Business Analysis. While these certifications require an investment, they signal a high level of commitment and competence to potential employers and can significantly enhance your profile. In the competitive field of business analysis, these certifications can serve as key differentiators in your career advancement, underscoring your expertise and dedication to the profession.

Regardless of the path you choose, remember that the primary goal is to keep learning and expanding your professional skill set. With these resources at your fingertips, you're well equipped to make your mark in the business analysis field.

Business Analyst Job Interview

The interview process for a Business Analyst position is not solely focused on assessing your technical skills but also aims to gauge if you align with the company's culture and values. Preparing effectively by understanding the job description and practicing your responses to common questions can significantly enhance your chances of success.

A Business Analyst interview often encompasses various categories of questions, including General, Technical, Behavioral, Situational, Role-specific, and Domain-specific. Below, we delve into these categories and provide examples that you might encounter.

1. General Interview Questions

These questions help interviewers understand your background, experience, and motivations. Preparing solid answers to these questions can set a positive tone for the rest of the interview.

- Why did you decide to become a Business Analyst?

- Can you describe your ideal work environment?

- What are your career goals as a Business Analyst?

- How do you handle feedback and criticism?

2. Technical Questions

Technical questions evaluate your knowledge and skills related to business analysis tools, methodologies, and practices.

- Can you explain what a use case is and how to create one?

- What business intelligence tools or data analysis software are you experienced with?

- What is your approach to handling large datasets?

3. Behavioural Questions

These questions explore how you act in specific workplace scenarios, reflecting your work style and problem-solving abilities.

- Tell me about a challenging project you worked on and how you managed it.

- Can you provide an example of a time when you showed initiative?

- How have you handled a situation when a project was not going as planned?

4. Situational/Case Study Questions

Situational questions present hypothetical situations/case studies to see how you might respond to challenges and unexpected events on the job.

- Suppose a stakeholder changes their requirements midway through the project. How would you handle it?

- How would you resolve a disagreement between two stakeholders about a requirement?

- If you were faced with a problem that you've never encountered before, how would you approach it?

- A case study might be presented that gives details of the situation and questions are asked to assess how you use your Business Analysis skills to tackle it.

5. Role-specific Questions

These inquiries zero in on your understanding of the business analyst role, expectations, and related responsibilities.

- What is your process for gathering and documenting business requirements?

- How would you conduct a feasibility study for a new project?

- What steps do you take to ensure that a project's scope is well-defined?

6. Domain-specific Questions

If the role pertains to a specific industry (such as healthcare, finance, or IT), you may face questions relevant to that domain.

- How have you used technology to improve business processes?

- What is your experience with data privacy and security?

- What do you consider the most challenging aspect of integrating IT systems within business operations?

The goal of a Business Analyst interview is multifaceted, assessing not only your technical prowess but also your fit within the company's culture. Researching the company, understanding the role, and having examples ready from your experience can help you feel prepared and confident.

To successfully answer these questions, many candidates utilize the STAR method, an effective strategy to articulate your experiences and skills:

- **Situation:** Describe the situation you were in.

- **Task:** Explain the task you were faced with.

- **Action:** Detail the action you took to address the task.

- **Result:** Share the result of your action, focusing on positive outcomes and what you learned.

For example, in response to a behavioural question like "Tell me about a challenging project you worked on and how you managed it," you can use the STAR method to structure your answer clearly and compellingly. By doing so, you'll demonstrate not only your aptitude for the job but also your ability to reflect on your experiences and articulate them in an insightful way.

Special Consideration for Different Levels

- **For Senior Business Analysts:** Be ready to discuss leadership experiences, stakeholder management techniques, and different project methodologies. Expect more complex technical and situational questions.

- **For Graduate Business Analysts**: Prepare to discuss academic projects, internships, coursework, and demonstrate your eagerness to learn. Questions may focus more on theoretical knowledge and potential rather than experience.

Now, we will shift our attention to two individualized and in-depth examples that further illuminate the interview process for distinct career stages. First, we will present an Interview with sample answers of a seasoned Senior Business Analyst who is preparing for a role in a leading tech company. Following that, we will delve into an Interview with answers of an ambitious Graduate Business Analyst as they prepare for their first full-time role. These interviews will provide concrete insights into the tailored preparation required for different levels within the Business Analyst profession. The interview process for a Business Analyst position is not just about technical know-how; it's a comprehensive evaluation of how you align with the company's culture and values. By understanding the specific job description and practicing your responses to common questions, you can significantly enhance your chances of success. The forthcoming interviews will offer a firsthand look at this process, highlighting the nuances and intricacies that define the path to becoming a successful Business Analyst.

.

Real Life Interview and answers of a seasoned Senior Business Analyst

For this interview we would consider the below Sample Job Description:

Business Analyst - Leeds/Hybrid - £36,333-£43,155 - Exceptional Benefits

We are delighted to be partnering with the University of Leeds, one of the top 135 universities in the world! The university are implementing a new digital strategy outlining ambitious plans to enhance student education, research and corporate systems and processes through the increased use of digital technology, data, and digital approaches.

Following the launch of the university's digital transformation strategy, they are laying out plans for modernising and securing their IT services to ensure they can support their digital future. As part of this we are looking to speak with experienced Business Analysts to join the organisation and contribute to their digital transformation journey.

In this position you will contribute to a wide variety of activities including, business process modelling, eliciting and documenting user stories, acceptance criteria, requirements and capturing business/technical data. Alongside developing new products for the client from inception to delivery with go-live dates in the pipeline to enhance customer experience across the organisation.

Key experience

2+ years as a Business Analyst

Demonstrable experience of business process mapping and modelling.

Excellent stakeholder management skill.

Strong problem-solving capability.

Demonstrable experience of working with system developers or suppliers.

What's in it for you?

This is an excellent opportunity for a Business Analyst to play a role in an industry leading transformation programme. You will be joining them at such a turning point in their evolution is a truly exciting opportunity.

You will be offered an unrivalled pension contribution and 26 days holiday plus approx.16 Bank Holidays/days the University is closed by custom (including Christmas) - 42 days a year!

Interview Questions with Sample Answers:

1. **General Interview Questions**: These are common interview questions that help interviewers understand your background, experience, and motivations.

Tell me about yourself?

I'm Richard Baker, a Business Analyst with over 5 years of professional experience in the field. I specialize in analyzing and improving business processes, and I'm passionate about using technology to drive efficiencies and growth.

I obtained my Bachelor's degree in Economics from Amazing University in Turkey. After graduation, I started my career as a Business Analyst at CyanGate in Turkey, where I worked on the improvement of retail workflows by implementing a Product Information Management (PIM) system.

Then, I moved to London and worked for Motivity Labs Inc., where I worked on an automated financing model for a consumer finance company. Here, I helped gather requirements and conducted gap analysis for process improvement initiatives.

Most recently, I worked at V Group Inc., where I was involved in the implementation of a payment management portal for a law firm. This role gave me the opportunity to work closely with cross-functional teams and offshore IT teams to implement new technology and systems.

One of my significant achievements includes implementing a process automation initiative that resulted in a 20% reduction in execution time and increased overall customer satisfaction. I take great pride in these accomplishments, and I'm eager to bring my skills and experience to new challenges.

My professional experiences have given me a well-rounded skill set, including first-rate analytical and problem-solving abilities. I'm also highly proficient in business process analysis and improvement, requirement gathering and documentation, and data analysis.

I'm eager to bring my technical skills, strategic mindset, and passion for innovation to the University of Leeds as it embarks on its digital transformation journey. I'm excited about the opportunity to work with a world-class institution and contribute to its digital future.

Can you give us a 2 min walkthrough of your resume?

I began my career as a Business Analyst in 2018 at CyanGate, a technology firm in Turkey. Here, I worked on enhancing retail workflows by enabling a Product Information Management system for Auto-Tagging. I served as the liaison between business stakeholders and IT teams, translating business requirements into technical specifications, and contributing to Agile project teams.

In 2020, I moved to the United States and joined Motivity Labs Inc. I was part of a team working on an automated financing model for a consumer finance company. My roles here varied from assisting in gathering requirements, conducting gap analysis, participating in Agile Scrum meetings, to supporting user acceptance testing. I had the privilege of managing projects and serving as the primary liaison between the client and multiple internal groups.

Most recently, I was with V Group Inc. in London, where I worked on the implementation of a payment management portal for a law firm. My responsibilities included conducting thorough analysis of business processes, creating requirement documents, and facilitating the agile development process. One of my most significant achievements here was acting as a key player in the successful implementation of the new payment system, which improved data accuracy and efficiency in customer relationship management.

Throughout my career, I've honed my skills in business process analysis and improvement, requirement gathering, data interpretation, project management, and Agile methodologies, among others. I believe these experiences and skills make me well-suited for the Business Analyst role at the University of Leeds.

My aim now is to leverage my expertise and analytical skills to contribute to your digital transformation journey. I'm eager to apply my experience of integrating IT solutions into business strategies to enhance the digital capabilities of the University.

Can you tell me a bit about yourself?

I'm Richard Baker, a Business Analyst with a keen interest in driving business growth and success through thoughtful analysis and process improvement. I am originally from Turkey, where I received my Bachelor's degree in Economics from Amazing University. I'm currently based in London.

Over the past five years, I've had the opportunity to work with diverse teams across different industries, which has allowed me to acquire a comprehensive understanding of business operations and develop a diverse set of skills. This includes business process analysis and improvement, requirements gathering and documentation, data interpretation, and project management.

In my previous roles, I've worked on significant projects, including the implementation of a payment management portal at V Group Inc., an automated financing model at Motivity Labs Inc., and the improvement of retail workflows at CyanGate, LLC. In these projects, I effectively served as the liaison between business stakeholders and IT teams, translating business requirements into technical specifications.

Outside work, I have a love for travel and exploring new cultures, and I also enjoy reading books related to economics and technology. These hobbies allow me to gain different perspectives, which I find incredibly valuable in my line of work.

I'm excited about the possibility of bringing my expertise and passion for business analysis to the University of Leeds to contribute to its digital transformation journey.

Why did you decide to become a Business Analyst? What do you like about being a Business Analyst?

I decided to become a Business Analyst because of my interest in economics and business processes, which I developed during my undergraduate studies. I found that being a Business Analyst offered the perfect blend of strategic thinking, problem-solving, and technology application, which are areas that I am truly passionate about.

As a Business Analyst, I enjoy the challenge of understanding business needs and translating them into technical solutions. It's like solving a puzzle where you need to fit the pieces together to form a complete picture. I also love the interaction with different stakeholders, from understanding their needs to helping them realize the potential of technology in addressing their concerns.

Moreover, the role is very dynamic, and no two days are the same. I constantly find myself learning and growing, be it new methodologies, tools, or industry trends. The variety and pace of work keep me engaged and motivated.

But most importantly, it is extremely rewarding to see how my work contributes to improving a business's operations and achieving its strategic objectives. Knowing that I can make a difference in helping an organization succeed is one of the most fulfilling aspects of being a Business Analyst.

Why do you want to work for our company? What interests you about our company? What do you know about our company?

The University of Leeds stands out for me due to its international reputation for excellence in education and research. I have always admired its dedication to providing top-tier educational experiences and fostering innovative research environments. It's exciting to think that I could play a role in supporting such a crucial mission.

What drew me to this opportunity is the university's ambitious digital strategy. It's clear that the university understands the importance of digital technology and data in enhancing student education and streamlining research and corporate systems. Being part of this digital transformation journey, not just as an observer, but as a contributor, is a prospect I find incredibly compelling.

I'm particularly interested in the project that involves business process modelling, capturing business/technical data, and developing new products. These areas align well with my skills and expertise, and I'm excited about the chance to leverage these to enhance customer experiences across the university.

From my research, I understand that the University of Leeds is committed to a people-centric approach, focusing on creating an inclusive and collaborative culture. These are values I deeply resonate with and I'm eager to contribute to a team that values diversity and collaboration.

The commitment to professional development also stands out to me. I'm keen to continue learning and growing in my career, and it seems that the University of Leeds is an environment where this would be strongly supported.

In short, the combination of the challenging work, the values the university upholds, and the potential for professional growth make this an opportunity I am very enthusiastic about.

What are your strengths and weaknesses?

Regarding my strengths, I'd highlight three main areas. First, I have a strong ability to analyze complex problems and processes and break them down into manageable components. This skill has been key to driving efficiency and accuracy in my previous roles.

Second, I have an excellent understanding of business requirements and how to translate them into technical specifications. My roles at CyanGate, Motivity Labs Inc., and V Group Inc. have all involved being the bridge between the business and technical teams, and I've been commended for my ability to communicate effectively between these groups.

Finally, I'm proficient in Agile methodologies, which I believe is crucial in the modern tech landscape. I've been part of Agile project teams, contributing to sprint planning, backlog grooming, and sprint reviews, which has improved project delivery times and overall efficiency.

As for weaknesses, one area I'm continuously working on is my ability to delegate tasks. As someone who takes great pride in my work, I can sometimes find it difficult to delegate tasks to others as I tend to want to complete them myself to ensure they're done correctly. However, I understand that effective delegation is a crucial part of being a successful team member and leader, so I've been consciously working on trusting my teammates more and sharing responsibilities.

Can you describe your ideal work environment?

My ideal work environment is one that promotes a culture of collaboration and inclusivity. I thrive in settings where team members feel comfortable sharing ideas, providing feedback, and working together towards common goals. I believe that diverse perspectives and collaborative problem-solving often lead to the most effective and innovative solutions.

I also value an environment that encourages continuous learning and professional growth. In the rapidly evolving field of business analysis and technology, it's important to keep up with industry trends and new methodologies. So, a company that provides opportunities for ongoing learning, whether through training programs, workshops, or conferences, is very appealing to me.

Additionally, I appreciate a work environment that balances professionalism with a bit of fun. Regular team-building activities and a positive, supportive atmosphere can make a significant difference in employee morale and productivity.

Finally, I believe in a work culture that acknowledges and appreciates the effort and accomplishments of its employees. Recognition for a job well done not only boosts individual morale but also fosters a sense of ownership and pride in one's work.

In my research about the University of Leeds, it seems to align well with these values, which is one of the reasons why I'm particularly excited about the opportunity to join your team.

Where do you see yourself in five years?

Five years from now, I see myself in a position where I am continuously contributing to the strategic goals of the organization, ideally at a more senior level. I aim to be a leading Business Analyst who drives major initiatives and impacts the organization's overall success. I also envision myself managing and mentoring junior analysts, sharing the knowledge and skills I've gained throughout my career.

I'm particularly interested in the intersection of data analysis and business strategy, so I aim to gain more exposure and develop expertise in data-driven decision making. I see myself leveraging advanced analytics tools to make informed business decisions that contribute to the company's growth.

In the next five years, I also want to deepen my understanding of Agile methodologies and perhaps even gain certification as a Scrum Master. This aligns with my goal to become an effective leader in managing projects and teams.

Ultimately, I aim to be in a role where I am not only a contributor but also a thought leader, driving innovation and process improvements. My goal is to make a significant impact on the organization's success and be a key player in its digital transformation journey. And I believe that the role at the University of Leeds will provide me with the opportunities and experiences to achieve these goals.

What do you think about the role on offer?

I find the role of a Business Analyst at the University of Leeds to be extremely appealing and in line with my career aspirations. The position seems to provide an opportunity to make substantial contributions to the digital transformation journey of the university, which is an exciting prospect.

I appreciate the breadth of activities involved in the role, from business process modelling and capturing business/technical data to developing new products and enhancing customer experience across the organization. These responsibilities align well with my skills and experiences, making me confident in my ability to contribute effectively.

The role also appears to offer a good mix of technical work and interaction with different stakeholders, which suits my abilities and preferences. I have a proven track record in managing stakeholder expectations and translating business requirements into technical specifications, which I believe will be key in this role.

Lastly, the opportunity to be part of the university's ambitious digital strategy is enticing. It's clear that the university is not just keeping up with the digital age but actively leveraging it to enhance the services it provides. Being part of this forward-thinking approach is something I'm very interested in.

Overall, I believe this role presents a challenge that I'm ready for and excited about, and I look forward to potentially contributing to the University of Leeds' digital transformation strategy.

What do you consider your greatest accomplishment in your previous role?

One accomplishment that stands out is the implementation of a new payment system at V Group Inc. This project involved the creation of a payment management portal for facilitating end-user payments for a law firm. It was a significant initiative due to the complexity of the requirements and the impact it would have on the firm's operations.

I was heavily involved in all stages of the project, from initial requirements gathering to system implementation. My responsibilities included conducting detailed analysis of the existing business processes, collaborating with cross-functional teams to gather requirements, creating detailed requirement documents, and acting as a liaison between business stakeholders and offshore IT teams.

What made this project particularly challenging was that it involved several different stakeholder groups, each with its own requirements and expectations. But through effective stakeholder management and constant communication, I was able to ensure alignment and consensus.

The project was a success, resulting in improved data accuracy and increased efficiency in customer relationship management. It also led to a significant improvement in end-user satisfaction with the payment process. This achievement was a testament to the power of effective business analysis and cross-team collaboration, and it's something I'm really proud of.

It's the kind of impact I strive to make in every role I take on, and it's what I'm excited to bring to the Business Analyst position at the University of Leeds.

Why did you leave your last job?

Below is a response that frames leaving a job due to circumstances beyond your control in a positive light:

While I immensely enjoyed my role and the projects I was involved in at V Group Inc., my departure was the result of circumstances beyond my control. The project that I was hired for reached its conclusion and due to financial constraints, the company was unable to extend my contract. It was unfortunate, as I had formed great relationships with the team and was deeply involved in the work we were doing.

However, I believe that every change is an opportunity for growth. I took this as a chance to look for new roles where I can apply my skills and experience, like the one here at the University of Leeds. I'm particularly attracted to your ambitious digital transformation project and I'm eager to contribute to an organization with such a clear vision for its future.

Other way of responding to the question:

My decision to leave my last job at V Group Inc. was primarily driven by the desire for new challenges and opportunities for growth. While I greatly enjoyed my role and had a productive time there, I realized that I had reached a point where there was limited scope for further professional growth within the same role.

I was fortunate to work on several impactful projects and collaborate with an exceptional team at V Group. We achieved some significant milestones, such as the successful implementation of a new payment management portal. However, I'm now looking for a role that allows me to leverage my skills and experience on a larger scale and in a new context.

This position at the University of Leeds presents the kind of challenge I'm looking for. The university's digital transformation strategy is ambitious and impactful, and the chance to be a part of this journey is something I find truly exciting. I'm confident that this role will provide the opportunity for growth and new challenges that I'm seeking.

What are your career goals as a Business Analyst?

As a Business Analyst, my immediate career goal is to continue expanding my skill set and knowledge in areas such as advanced data analysis, AI applications in business, and agile project management methodologies. These skills are increasingly important in today's rapidly changing digital landscape, and I believe they will enable me to provide more strategic and impactful contributions.

In the medium-term, I aim to become a Senior Business Analyst or a Lead Business Analyst, where I would have the opportunity to manage more significant projects and perhaps mentor junior analysts. I believe that with my experience and continuous learning, I can advance into these roles and contribute even more to an organization's strategic goals.

My long-term career goal is to be in a position where I can drive the strategic direction of an organization through technology and process improvements. A role such as a Director of Business Analysis or a similar senior-level position would be my ultimate objective. In this capacity, I hope to influence an organization's decision-making process at the highest level, using data-driven insights to drive growth and improvement.

Throughout my career, regardless of the role I'm in, my goal is to continuously learn and adapt to the changing business landscape. I want to remain at the forefront of industry developments and best practices, so I can keep providing value to my team and the wider organization.

What do you consider your strengths? What about your weaknesses?

One of my key strengths is my analytical skills. Over the years, I've honed my ability to analyze complex data and information to identify key insights and drive strategic decisions. This skill has been crucial in various projects I've undertaken, such as the implementation of a payment management portal and the automation of a financing model.

I also excel in stakeholder management. I'm adept at understanding and navigating the diverse interests and concerns of various stakeholders. I've successfully liaised between business stakeholders and IT teams in my previous roles, ensuring smooth communication and effective translation of business requirements into technical specifications.

Another strength of mine is my proficiency in Agile methodologies. Having worked extensively in Agile environments, I'm familiar with the practices and principles that drive successful Agile projects, from sprint planning to backlog grooming and sprint reviews.

In terms of weaknesses, one area that I'm continually working on is my public speaking skills. While I'm comfortable in small group settings and one-on-one interactions, I can find larger presentations or public speaking engagements more challenging. I've been working to improve this by seeking out opportunities to present and speak in public. I've made considerable progress and plan to continue developing this skill.

Another area I'm looking to improve is my knowledge of advanced data analysis tools and techniques. As businesses become increasingly data-driven, I understand the importance of being proficient in the latest tools. So, I've been dedicating time to learning and mastering more advanced data analytics tools to improve my capabilities in this area.

How do you handle feedback and criticism?

I consider feedback and criticism to be essential components of personal and professional growth. I believe that every piece of feedback, whether positive or negative, is an opportunity to learn and improve.

When I receive criticism, I make an effort to listen carefully and understand the perspective of the person providing it. I don't rush to defend myself or my work, but rather take time to digest the feedback and assess its validity. If I'm unclear about any points, I ask for clarification to ensure I fully understand the feedback.

Once I've processed the feedback, I use it to inform my future actions and decisions. If there's a specific issue pointed out, I make a plan to address it and monitor my progress. For instance, if a team member suggests a different approach to a task, I try to incorporate their suggestion into my work and evaluate its effectiveness.

I also appreciate open dialogue and encourage people to provide feedback to me directly. I believe this open and direct communication fosters a culture of continuous improvement and helps teams perform at their best.

In conclusion, I view feedback and criticism positively and as essential tools for personal and professional development. They help me identify areas for improvement, refine my skills, and ultimately become a more effective Business Analyst.

2. **Technical Questions**: These questions assess your technical knowledge and skills related to business analysis.

Can you explain what a use case is and how to create one?

A use case is a tool used in system analysis to identify, clarify, and organize system requirements. It represents a specific way that a system can be used by an end user (also known as an actor) to accomplish a particular goal. Use cases are important because they help to clarify what the system needs to do, and they form a basis for the design, development, and testing of the system.

Creating a use case involves several steps:

1. Identify the Actors: The first step is to identify the actors involved in the process. An actor can be a person, another system, or an organization that interacts with the system. For example, in a banking application, the actors could include customers, bank employees, and the banking system itself.

2. Identify the Use Cases: The next step is to identify the use cases themselves. These represent the interactions between the actors and the system. In our banking example, use cases could include "Check Account Balance," "Deposit Money," "Withdraw Money," etc.

3. Define the Flow of Events: Once you've identified the use cases, the next step is to define the flow of events for each one. This is a detailed description of how the system interacts with the actor to achieve the goal of the use case. It's usually divided into two parts: the basic flow, which is the standard course of events when everything goes as expected, and the

alternative flows, which cover exceptional circumstances or errors.

4. Create Use Case Diagrams: Use case diagrams are graphical representations of the relationships between actors and use cases. They provide a high-level overview of how the system will be used.

5. Write Use Case Scenarios: Finally, use case scenarios are detailed, narrative descriptions of the use case. They describe the sequence of events from the perspective of the actor using the system, and they help ensure that all potential scenarios have been considered.

By creating use cases, you can ensure that all key interactions are identified and understood before system development begins, which leads to a more efficient and successful development process.

Can you explain the difference between Scrum and Waterfall methodologies?

Scrum and Waterfall are both methodologies used in project management, particularly in software development, but they are based on very different principles and processes.

Waterfall Methodology is a linear and sequential approach to project management. Projects are broken down into distinct stages that are completed one after another. Typically, these stages include requirements gathering, design, implementation, verification, and maintenance. Each stage must be completed before the next one begins, and there is typically little to no overlap between stages. Feedback is not usually incorporated until the testing or verification stage. This method works well for projects with clear, unchanging requirements and a predictable path to the outcome.

On the other hand, Scrum is a form of Agile methodology, which is iterative and flexible. Work is divided into small parts, known as "sprints", which typically last between 1 to 4 weeks. The focus is on continuous improvement and regular feedback. After each sprint, the team reviews the work and the process, adjusting as necessary for the next sprint. Scrum promotes close collaboration, regular communication, and quick response to changes. Scrum works well for projects where requirements are expected to change or evolve, and creativity and innovation are valued.

In summary, the key difference between Scrum and Waterfall lies in their approach to project management. Waterfall follows a linear and sequential process, and works best when requirements are known and fixed. In contrast, Scrum follows an iterative and flexible process, accommodating changes and revisions throughout the development process, making it ideal for projects where requirements may evolve over time.

How do you handle data validation?

Data validation is a critical step in any data analysis project or any project that involves the use of data. It's all about ensuring the data you're working with is accurate, consistent, and useful for your needs. Here are the steps I generally take to handle data validation:

1. Data Cleaning: The first step usually involves cleaning the data. This may include dealing with missing or null values,

correcting obvious errors, and standardizing or normalizing data so it's in a consistent and usable format.

2. Consistency Checks: I look for inconsistencies in the data. For example, if there's a field that should contain only numerical values, I'll check to ensure there are no non-numerical values present.

3. Range Checks: This involves checking that numerical values fall within an expected range. For instance, if we have a data field for 'age', values should realistically be between 0 and say, 120.

4. Unique Checks: For certain data fields, uniqueness might be important. For example, in a database of customers, each customer should ideally have a unique customer ID.

5. Cross-Checks: This involves cross-referencing data from different sources or fields to ensure consistency. If a piece of data is reported in two different places, it should match in both.

6. Utilizing Domain Knowledge: Domain knowledge can be used to further validate data. For instance, if we're looking at a retail sales dataset, we can expect higher sales around the holiday season. If we don't see this trend, it may indicate an issue with the data.

7. Use of Data Validation Tools: There are many data validation tools available that can automate much of this process. Depending on the complexity and volume of the data, I might use such tools to streamline the data validation process.

It's important to note that data validation is an ongoing process, not a one-time event. As new data comes in, or as the data is manipulated and analyzed, it's important to continue to validate the data to ensure it's accurate and reliable.

What business intelligence tools or data analysis software are you experienced with?

Throughout my career as a Business Analyst, I've had the opportunity to work with several business intelligence and data analysis tools that have been crucial in conducting comprehensive data analysis, generating insights, and making data-driven decisions.

1. Microsoft Excel: This is a fundamental tool I've used extensively for data manipulation, statistical analysis, and visualization. I've used advanced Excel features like PivotTables, VLOOKUP, and a variety of statistical functions.

2. SQL: SQL is essential for working with databases. I've used SQL to query databases, manipulate data, and generate custom reports.

3. Tableau: This is a powerful data visualization tool. I've used Tableau to create interactive dashboards and visualizations to present data in a more digestible and actionable format.

4. Power BI: Another BI tool that I've used to create interactive reports and dashboards, and to perform data modelling.

5. Python: I have some experience with Python for data analysis, particularly with libraries like pandas and numpy

for data manipulation and analysis, and matplotlib and seaborn for data visualization.

6. JIRA and Confluence: While these are more project management tools, they have been invaluable in my roles as a business analyst for tracking progress, documenting requirements, and facilitating communication within the team.

In addition to these, I've also worked with a variety of project management and collaboration tools, including Slack, Asana, and Trello. My familiarity with a variety of tools allows me to adapt quickly to the specific tools and technologies used by a particular organization.

Can you explain the concept of data modelling?

Data modelling is a process used to define and analyze data requirements that are necessary for supporting business processes within the scope of corresponding information systems. Essentially, it's a conceptual representation of data structures, relationships, rules, and constraints and is used to plan the organization of data.

Data modelling involves three stages:

1. Conceptual Data Model: This is the most abstract form of data model. It includes the important entities and the relationships among them. No attribute is specified in this level. It's used to communicate ideas and understand business needs.

2. Logical Data Model: This defines the structure of the data elements and sets the relationships between them. It

introduces details like attribute types (such as text, integer, decimal, etc.), primary and foreign keys and constraints while still not considering how this will be implemented in a specific database system.

3. Physical Data Model: This represents an application and database-specific implementation of a logical data model. It includes details such as how the data will be stored, retrieved, and updated in the database system, table names, column names, data types, and how they map to the real-world constructs that the database is designed to capture.

Data modelling helps to understand the information requirements, improve communication within the organization, provides a clear picture of the data that needs to be stored and accessed, and can be used as a blueprint for designing databases. The overall aim is to make sure data objects offered by the functional team are represented accurately.

Are you familiar with SQL or any other database query language?

Yes, I am familiar with SQL, which stands for Structured Query Language. SQL is a standard language for managing and manipulating relational databases. I have used SQL extensively in my previous roles as a business analyst to interact with databases.

My experience with SQL includes:

1. Data Retrieval: I've written SQL SELECT statements to retrieve data from databases, including complex queries

involving JOINs, WHERE clauses, GROUP BY clauses, and more.

2. Data Manipulation: I've used INSERT, UPDATE, and DELETE statements to add new records, change existing data, and remove records from databases.

3. Database Structure Manipulation: Although less common in my business analyst roles, I have experience using CREATE, ALTER, and DROP statements to create, change, and delete database structures like tables and views.

4. Data Aggregation: I've written queries to perform various aggregations on data, such as sums, averages, counts, minimums, and maximums, often in combination with GROUP BY statements.

5. Subqueries and Nested Queries: I've written complex SQL queries that include subqueries, nested queries, and common table expressions (CTEs) to manage complex data manipulation tasks.

6. Stored Procedures and Functions: Although I mostly worked with SQL queries, I have basic knowledge of creating and using stored procedures and functions, which allow for encapsulation and reuse of SQL code.

Overall, I am comfortable using SQL to interact with relational databases, and I consider it a key skill in my toolkit as a business analyst.

In which project have you used SQL?

During my tenure as a Business Analyst at V Group Inc., I frequently utilized SQL in a project to implement a payment management portal for a law firm. This project required extensive data manipulation and extraction to ensure that the payment system worked effectively and aligned with the business requirements of the law firm.

One of the key tasks involved creating a reporting system to keep track of all the payments being processed through the portal. I wrote complex SQL queries to extract relevant data from various tables in our database, involving multiple joins, filters, and aggregation functions.

For instance, I created SQL queries that helped the firm identify the total amount of payments received within specific timeframes, segregated by various categories such as payment method, type of legal service, and so forth. These reports were crucial for the law firm's financial analysis and helped them identify trends and opportunities for improving their service offering.

In addition, I used SQL scripts to perform regular data validation and cleanup tasks. This included identifying and rectifying inconsistencies in the data, ensuring that all payments were properly recorded, and that customer data was accurate and up-to-date

This experience not only deepened my SQL skills, but also underscored the importance of clear, efficient data management in supporting business decisions and operations. SQL was instrumental in the success of this project and has been a valuable tool in my career as a Business Analyst.

What is your experience with project management tools, such as JIRA or MS Project?

I have considerable experience with various project management tools, each of which has played an important role in different projects I've worked on.

1. JIRA: I have used JIRA extensively during my tenure at V Group Inc. and Motivity Labs Inc. It was the primary tool we used for managing our Agile development processes. I've used it to create and track user stories and tasks, plan sprints, and manage backlogs. I've also used JIRA to monitor project progress, track bugs, and manage issues. Furthermore, I've used it as a communication tool to collaborate with other team members and ensure that everyone is updated with the latest information.

2. MS Project: In my previous roles, I've used MS Project to create project schedules, assign resources to tasks, track project progress, manage budgets, and analyze workloads. It was a critical tool for our team when we worked on larger projects that involved several resources and dependencies.

3. Confluence: Alongside JIRA, I've used Confluence for creating and maintaining project documentation, knowledge sharing, and collaboration. Confluence was particularly helpful in capturing the history and context of our project decisions, creating a shared understanding among team members, and keeping everyone aligned on project goals and requirements.

4. Trello and Asana: For less complex projects, I've used Trello and Asana as simpler project management tools. They've been especially helpful for visualizing task progress, managing workflows, and facilitating collaboration among team members.

Each of these tools has its strengths, and the choice of tool often depends on the nature and complexity of the project. Regardless of the specific tool, I believe that effective use of project management software is crucial for keeping projects on track and ensuring effective communication and collaboration within the team.

Can you describe how to perform a SWOT analysis?

SWOT analysis is a strategic planning technique that's used to help an individual or organization identify their Strengths, Weaknesses, Opportunities, and Threats related to competition or project planning. Here is how it's typically performed:

1. Strengths: First, you identify your strengths. These are the internal positive attributes, resources, or capabilities that give you an advantage over others. It could be anything from strong financial resources, a dedicated team, a unique product, a strong brand, etc. You should ask, what advantages do you have? What do you do better than anyone else?

2. Weaknesses: Next, you determine your weaknesses. These are also internal factors that might put you at a disadvantage relative to others. This could include things like lack of resources, inexperienced team, poor location, etc. The key is

to be honest about what might be holding you back. What areas need improvement to accomplish your objectives or compete with your strongest competitor?

3. Opportunities: Now, you look externally to identify opportunities. These are the conditions outside your organization that could potentially be advantageous. It could be a growing market, an unserved customer segment, technological advancements, and more. Are there trends or changes in the market that you can leverage? What opportunities are available to you?

4. Threats: Lastly, you consider the threats. These are external factors that could potentially harm you. It could be things like growing competition, changes in regulatory environment, market decline, etc. What obstacles do you face? Are there competitors who could pose a threat?

By conducting a SWOT analysis, you can get a comprehensive view of your strategic position. The aim is to use your strengths to take advantage of the opportunities and to reduce the impact of weaknesses and protect against threats. This will help you make more informed decisions and develop a strategic plan that takes all of these factors into account.

What is your approach to handling large datasets?

Handling large datasets effectively requires a combination of robust tools, appropriate techniques, and a systematic approach. Here's how I typically handle large datasets:

1. Understanding the Data: My first step when dealing with large datasets is to gain a thorough understanding of the data.

What does each column represent? What kind of data does it contain? How is it structured? This understanding is crucial for determining how to approach the data and what kind of analysis might be useful.

2. Data Cleaning and Preparation: Large datasets often contain incomplete, inconsistent, or irrelevant parts of data that can distort your analysis. Cleaning the data is a crucial step in the process and may involve dealing with missing data, identifying and correcting errors, removing duplicates, and standardizing and categorizing data.

3. Data Reduction: In some cases, the dataset may contain more information than is needed for the analysis. In such cases, I use techniques like dimensionality reduction or sampling to simplify the data while retaining its essential features.

4. Data Analysis Tools: I use robust data analysis tools that can handle large datasets efficiently. For example, SQL for data extraction and manipulation, Python libraries like Pandas for data analysis, and Tableau for data visualization. These tools are specifically designed to work with large datasets and can help make the process more manageable.

5. Automation: Wherever possible, I automate processes to improve efficiency. This might include writing scripts to automate data cleaning or setting up automated data import/export processes.

6. Performance Considerations: When working with large datasets, it's important to consider the performance impact of your data handling processes. This might mean optimizing

your SQL queries, using more efficient data structures, or implementing parallel processing where appropriate.

7. Data Security and Privacy: Large datasets often contain sensitive information. It's essential to ensure that the data is stored and handled securely, and that privacy considerations are respected, including compliance with relevant regulations.

By taking a systematic, tool-based approach and applying appropriate techniques, I can effectively handle large datasets and extract meaningful insights from them.

How do you ensure the quality of your data?

Ensuring data quality is a crucial part of any analysis, as the insights and decisions derived from the data are only as good as the data itself. Here's my approach to ensuring data quality:

1. Data Collection: It starts at the data collection stage, where I ensure that the data collection methods are sound and reliable. This involves clearly defining what data is to be collected, how it is to be measured, and ensuring the sources of the data are credible.

2. Data Cleaning: After collection, the data must be cleaned. This process includes identifying and handling missing values, removing duplicates, correcting inconsistencies, and handling outliers. I use various tools and techniques for data cleaning, such as SQL for data manipulation, and Python libraries like Pandas for data cleaning and preparation.

3. Validation Checks: I use validation checks to ensure data is accurate and consistent. These checks could include range checks to ensure the data falls within the expected range, consistency checks to ensure data across different fields or records is consistent, and uniqueness checks to ensure that data that should be unique, is unique.

4. Automated Data Quality Tools: There are numerous data quality tools available that can automate many aspects of data quality assurance. These tools can perform tasks such as data profiling, which helps understand the data, validate rules, which check data for consistency, and monitoring, which ensures data quality is maintained over time.

5. Data Auditing: Periodic data audits are crucial to maintaining data quality over time. These audits involve checking the data for accuracy, completeness, and consistency, identifying any issues, and correcting them.

6. Creating a Data Dictionary: A data dictionary provides a description of the data, detailing what each column represents, the type of data it contains, acceptable values or range of values, and any relationships with other data fields. This is a crucial tool for maintaining data quality, as it provides a clear understanding of what the data should look like.

7. Training and Education: Finally, ensuring data quality isn't just a technical issue; it's also about people. I believe in promoting a culture that values data quality, which includes training and educating staff on the importance of data quality and how to achieve it.

By adopting these measures, I strive to ensure that the data I work with is of the highest quality, thereby enabling accurate and reliable analysis and decision-making.

3. **Behavioural Questions**: These questions help the interviewer understand how you behave in specific workplace situations based on your past experiences.

Can you describe a time when you had to manage a difficult stakeholder?

In my previous role as a Business Analyst at CyanGate, I encountered a challenging stakeholder during the implementation of a Product Information Management (PIM) system for retail workflows. This stakeholder, a senior executive from the marketing department, had reservations about the proposed changes and was resistant to embracing the new system.

To effectively manage this difficult stakeholder, I took the following steps:

1. Active Listening and Empathy: I initiated one-on-one meetings with the stakeholder to understand their concerns and perspectives. I actively listened to their feedback, allowing them to express their reservations openly. By demonstrating empathy and understanding their point of view, I created an environment where they felt heard and valued.

2. Effective Communication: I ensured clear and frequent communication to keep the stakeholder informed about the benefits and impacts of the new system. I shared relevant

239

documentation, such as business cases and success stories from similar implementations, to address their concerns and build confidence in the proposed changes.

3. Addressing Concerns: I proactively addressed the stakeholder's specific concerns and challenges related to the PIM system. I worked closely with the implementation team and other stakeholders to develop tailored solutions and mitigations that aligned with the stakeholder's requirements and business objectives. This involved adjusting the system configuration, providing additional training, and offering ongoing support.

4. Building Trust: Building trust was crucial in managing this difficult stakeholder. I consistently delivered on my commitments, provided transparent updates, and showcased the positive impacts of the PIM system on other retail workflows. By demonstrating competence, reliability, and integrity, I gradually built trust with the stakeholder and alleviated their concerns.

5. Collaboration and Compromise: I fostered a collaborative approach, involving the stakeholder in the decision-making process and seeking their input on key aspects of the implementation. I acknowledged their expertise and insights, and we worked together to find mutually beneficial solutions. Where necessary, I was willing to compromise and adapt the implementation plan to accommodate their requirements, ensuring a sense of ownership and investment from their side.

Through these efforts, I successfully managed the difficult stakeholder's resistance and skepticism. Over time, they became more receptive to the changes and actively contributed to the project's success. The stakeholder's support ultimately played a vital role in driving the adoption of the PIM system and realizing the desired improvements in retail workflows.

Tell me about a challenging project you worked on and how you managed it.

One of the challenging projects I worked on was the implementation of an automated financing model for a consumer finance company during my time at Motivity Labs Inc. The goal was to develop a system that could streamline the financing process and improve overall operational efficiency

Here's how I managed the project:

1. Thorough Requirement Gathering: I conducted extensive requirement gathering sessions with stakeholders from different departments to ensure a comprehensive understanding of their needs and pain points. This involved engaging with business users, IT teams, and senior management to identify and prioritize requirements.

2. Effective Project Planning: With a clear understanding of the project requirements, I created a detailed project plan, outlining key milestones, deliverables, and timelines. I allocated resources appropriately, considering the expertise and availability of team members, to ensure smooth execution of tasks.

3. Cross-Functional Collaboration: As the project involved multiple stakeholders, including business users, IT teams, and finance professionals, I facilitated effective collaboration and communication among all parties. Regular meetings, workshops, and progress updates were conducted to ensure everyone remained aligned and any potential roadblocks were addressed promptly.

4. Managing Scope and Change: During the project, scope creep and changing requirements were challenges we faced. To manage this, I implemented a change management process that involved assessing the impact of proposed changes, evaluating their feasibility, and involving relevant stakeholders in the decision-making process. This allowed us to prioritize changes effectively and maintain project focus.

5. Risk Identification and Mitigation: I conducted thorough risk assessments throughout the project lifecycle. This involved identifying potential risks and their potential impact on project deliverables, timelines, and budget. By proactively addressing risks, such as system integrations, data quality issues, or resource constraints, I developed mitigation strategies to minimize their impact and ensure project success.

6. Regular Progress Tracking and Reporting: To maintain transparency and accountability, I implemented a robust progress tracking and reporting mechanism. This included regular status updates, milestone reviews, and progress dashboards that provided stakeholders with clear visibility into project progress, risks, and mitigation efforts.

7. User Acceptance Testing and Training: To ensure successful adoption of the automated financing model, I facilitated user acceptance testing sessions to gather feedback from end-users and address any issues or usability concerns. I also coordinated training sessions to equip users with the necessary knowledge and skills to utilize the system effectively.

By applying effective project management techniques, maintaining open communication, and adapting to evolving project dynamics, we successfully delivered the automated financing model. The project resulted in improved operational efficiency, reduced processing time, and enhanced customer experience for the consumer finance company.

Have you ever made a mistake at work? How did you handle it?

In my early tenure at V Group Inc., we were in the process of implementing a new payment management portal. I made a mistake in underestimating the amount of time needed for certain aspects of the project, particularly the time needed for user acceptance testing. This caused a delay in our project timeline.

Once I realized the error, I immediately brought it to the attention of my project manager and the rest of the team. I took responsibility for the oversight and presented a revised schedule, which included a more accurate estimate of the remaining work. To address the delay, I suggested working on parallel tasks where possible and bringing in additional resources if necessary.

I learned a valuable lesson from this experience. It taught me the importance of careful and conservative project estimation, as well as the value of transparency and open communication when problems arise. Since then, I have improved my time estimation skills and have not repeated the same mistake in subsequent projects.

How do you handle conflicts within your team?

Handling conflicts within a team is a delicate process and requires understanding, communication, and sometimes, mediation.

While working on the payment management portal at V Group Inc., I encountered a situation where two of our team members had a disagreement about the approach to a particular requirement implementation. One team member wanted to use a more traditional approach which had been tested and proven, while the other was keen on trying a new method that was more innovative but less tested.

Rather than letting this disagreement turn into a bigger issue, I decided to step in and resolve the conflict. First, I arranged a meeting with both individuals to openly discuss their perspectives. I ensured both team members had an equal opportunity to present their viewpoints.

After both sides were presented, I facilitated a discussion around the pros and cons of each approach, focusing on the overall project requirements, deadlines, and risk appetite. We collectively decided to go with the traditional approach due to time constraints but agreed to revisit the new method for future projects, acknowledging the potential it held for innovation and improvement.

This experience taught me that when dealing with conflicts, it's crucial to foster open dialogue, ensure everyone feels heard, and focus on making decisions that are in the best interest of the project and team.

Can you provide an example of a time when you showed initiative?

During my tenure with Motivity Labs, I was working on an automated financing model for a consumer finance company. While working on this project, I noticed a potential bottleneck in the way data was being processed, which was not part of my assigned responsibility but was causing delays in my work.

Recognizing the impact of this issue on our timeline, I took the initiative to investigate the problem. I spent some time outside of my regular duties researching the issue and developing a proposal to optimize the data processing workflow.

I then approached my project manager, explained the situation, the potential impact on our project, and my proposed solution. After getting the approval, I worked with the relevant teams to implement the optimization. As a result, we were able to reduce data processing time and keep the project on track.

This experience reinforced my belief in being proactive and seeking opportunities to improve processes, even when they fall outside of my immediate responsibilities.

Tell me about a time you had to explain a complex subject to a non-technical stakeholder.

During my time with V Group Inc., we were implementing a new payment management portal for a law firm. One of the critical stakeholders was a senior partner at the firm who wasn't tech-savvy but had a keen interest in understanding the functionality and benefits of the new system.

It was important to explain the technical aspects and benefits of the system in a language that was easily understandable. Instead of going into the technical jargon, I chose to explain the project using a simplified analogy. I compared the payment management portal to a multi-lane highway, where each lane represents a different payment method, and the toll booths are the verification and validation checks in the system.

By using this analogy, I was able to explain the complexity of the payment portal, how it processes multiple payments simultaneously, and its ability to validate and verify payments quickly and efficiently.

The senior partner appreciated the explanation and was able to understand the system's workings better. This situation taught me the importance of adapting my communication style to the audience's needs and knowledge level to ensure effective communication.

How have you handled a situation when a project was not going as planned?

During my tenure at CyanGate, I was leading the implementation of a Product Information Management (PIM) system for Auto-Tagging in retail workflows. Midway through the project, we found out that the chosen PIM system wasn't integrating well with the existing systems as planned, causing significant delays.

The first step I took was to conduct an impact assessment to understand the extent of the issue and how it would affect our project timeline, budget, and resources. Once we had a clear understanding of the problem, I communicated the situation to the project stakeholders, ensuring transparency.

We then convened a meeting with the core project team to brainstorm possible solutions. These included exploring alternative methods of integration, liaising with the PIM system's vendor for support, or considering a different PIM system. We evaluated each solution based on impact, feasibility, and time requirements.

The decided course of action was to work closely with the PIM system's vendor. This decision was made considering the cost and time involved in transitioning to a new system, along with the vendor's willingness to assist in the situation.

Throughout this process, I kept all stakeholders updated and adjusted our project plan to accommodate these unforeseen circumstances. It was a challenging situation, but it taught me the importance of flexibility, quick problem-solving, and transparent communication in project management.

Can you provide an example of when you had to make a critical decision under pressure?

During my tenure at CyanGate, I was leading the implementation of a Product Information Management (PIM) system for Auto-Tagging in retail workflows. Midway through the project, we found out that the chosen PIM system wasn't integrating well with the existing systems as planned, causing significant delays.

The first step I took was to conduct an impact assessment to understand the extent of the issue and how it would affect our project timeline, budget, and resources. Once we had a clear understanding of the problem, I communicated the situation to the project stakeholders, ensuring transparency.

We then convened a meeting with the core project team to brainstorm possible solutions. These included exploring alternative methods of integration, liaising with the PIM system's vendor for support, or considering a different PIM system. We evaluated each solution based on impact, feasibility, and time requirements.

The decided course of action was to work closely with the PIM system's vendor. This decision was made considering the cost and time involved in transitioning to a new system, along with the vendor's willingness to assist in the situation.

Throughout this process, I kept all stakeholders updated and adjusted our project plan to accommodate these unforeseen circumstances. It was a challenging situation, but it taught me the importance of flexibility, quick problem-solving, and transparent communication in project management.

Describe a situation where you used data to drive a business strategy.

During my time at V Group Inc., I was assigned to implement a payment management portal for a law firm. While the primary goal was to facilitate smoother payments, I saw an opportunity to use the payment data to influence our client's business strategy.

We were generating a substantial amount of data from the new system, including the frequency of payments, the most common payment methods, the average transaction amount, and time of most payments. I proposed a strategy to analyze this data and provide valuable insights to the firm.

After conducting a comprehensive data analysis, we found trends like higher payment activity during the first and last weeks of the month and a significant preference for online payments over traditional methods.

I presented these findings to the firm, suggesting a strategy based on the data. I recommended that they could schedule their billing cycles to coincide with the times when clients were most likely to make payments and consider incentivizing online payments to further improve efficiency.

The firm implemented these suggestions and found them very effective in increasing their collections and enhancing their client service. This situation demonstrated the value of data in influencing business strategies and decisions.

Can you tell me about a time when you had to go above and beyond to get the job done?

I can share an instance from my tenure at Motivity Labs Inc. I was involved in developing an automated financing model for a consumer finance company. While we were working on this project, we came across a set of complicated technical issues that were proving to be a roadblock for our development team.

Though as a Business Analyst, troubleshooting technical issues wasn't within my primary responsibilities, the project was critical and on a tight deadline. Understanding the gravity of the situation and the potential delay in our project, I decided to step in.

Leveraging my understanding of the project requirements and technical aspects, I worked late hours alongside the development team to comprehend the issue and explore potential solutions. I coordinated with external technical consultants, sought their expertise, and relayed their guidance to our internal team.

Through this intensive collaborative effort, we were able to resolve the issues and keep the project on track. Though it required going beyond my usual responsibilities and putting in extra time, seeing the project succeed and our client satisfied was absolutely worth the effort.

This experience further emphasized the importance of flexibility, teamwork, and commitment to achieving project goals, no matter the challenges.

4. **Situational Questions**: These questions present hypothetical situations to gauge how you might handle certain scenarios on the job.

Suppose a stakeholder changes their requirements midway through the project. How would you handle it?

Changes in requirements midway through a project can be challenging, but they are often part of the reality of project management, especially in Agile environments. It's important to manage such changes in a way that minimizes disruption to the project and aligns all stakeholders on the new direction.

During my time at CyanGate, we faced a similar situation while working on a Product Information Management (PIM) system for Auto-Tagging in retail workflows. The client decided to change some of their requirements midway, which had a potential impact on our project timeline and delivery.

Here's how I handled it:

1. Clarify and Understand the Changes: First, I scheduled a meeting with the stakeholder to understand the proposed changes in detail and their reasons for the adjustments. This step was crucial to ensure we were on the same page about what the new requirements were and why they were necessary.

2. Impact Analysis: Once the new requirements were clear, my team and I conducted an impact analysis to understand how these changes would affect the project timeline, budget, and resources. This included looking at potential technical

challenges, the extra time needed for implementation, and any additional costs.

3. Communicate the Impact: I then shared the impact analysis with the stakeholder, making sure they were aware of the potential implications of the changes on the project. In this case, it meant extending the project timeline and increasing the budget.

4. Reach a Consensus: After discussing the implications, we worked together to reach a consensus. The client understood the trade-offs and agreed to extend the project timeline and adjust the budget to accommodate the new requirements.

5. Adjust the Project Plan: We then adjusted the project plan accordingly, redefined tasks, allocated new resources where necessary, and communicated the new project plan to all project team members and stakeholders.

By tackling the change in a structured and transparent manner, we were able to smoothly integrate the new requirements into our project without causing significant disruption.

How would you resolve a disagreement between two stakeholders about a requirement?

Resolving disagreements between stakeholders is an important aspect of a Business Analyst's role. It requires diplomacy, good listening skills, and the ability to find a solution that best aligns with the project goals.

During my time at V Group Inc., I had to mediate a situation where two key stakeholders had differing opinions on a feature for the payment management portal we were developing. One stakeholder believed the feature was critical for user experience, while the other was concerned about the additional time and cost involved in implementing it.

Here's how I approached the situation:

1. Understand Each Perspective: I first held separate meetings with each stakeholder to understand their points of view thoroughly. This allowed me to understand the reasoning behind their opinions without the pressure of an opposing viewpoint in the same conversation.

2. Find Common Ground: The next step was to identify any commonalities between their viewpoints. Both stakeholders agreed that user experience was important, but differed on the cost and time implications.

3. Facilitate a Discussion: I arranged a meeting with both stakeholders present. We discussed the importance of user experience, cost, and project timelines. I acted as a neutral party, ensuring each person had an opportunity to express their concerns and thoughts.

4. Propose a Compromise: Based on their inputs, I suggested a middle ground – to design a scaled-down version of the feature. This would address the user experience concern without significantly impacting the cost and timeline.

5. Make a Decision: With the agreement of both stakeholders on this compromise, we revised the project scope to include the scaled-down feature.

This experience reaffirmed that when resolving disagreements, it's essential to ensure all parties feel heard and respected, and that the final decision aligns with the project's best interests.

Imagine you're assigned to a project with a very tight deadline. How would you ensure it's completed on time?

Working under tight deadlines can be challenging but with the right approach, it's possible to ensure the project is completed on time. Here's how I'd approach this situation, drawing from my experience as a Business Analyst:

1. Clear Understanding: Firstly, I would ensure I have a comprehensive understanding of the project, its scope, and specific deliverables. It's crucial to know exactly what needs to be achieved to manage time effectively.

2. Prioritize Tasks: Not all tasks are of equal importance. Some are critical to the project while others, though important, might not have an immediate impact on the project's progression. By prioritizing tasks based on their urgency and importance, I can ensure that the critical path of the project is not delayed.

3. Create a Detailed Project Plan: Having a well-structured project plan is key to managing tight deadlines. I would outline all the tasks, allocate resources, and set a timeline for each task. This plan would provide a clear path to follow and help track the progress.

4. Allocate Resources Efficiently: Ensuring that tasks are assigned to team members based on their skills and capacities

is crucial. This not only helps in efficient execution but also boosts morale as team members are working on tasks they are competent in.

5. Frequent Check-ins: Regular status updates and check-ins with the team would help identify any potential roadblocks or delays in the project. This proactive approach would allow us to tackle issues before they can significantly impact the project timeline.

6. Flexibility: Despite careful planning, unforeseen issues can arise. Being flexible and ready to adapt the plan as necessary is essential.

7. Risk Management: Identifying potential risks in advance and having mitigation strategies in place can prevent surprises that could cause delays.

For instance, while working on the automated financing model at Motivity Labs Inc., we had a tight deadline. By employing these strategies, we were able to meet the deadline without compromising the quality of our work.

If you found out that a project was going off track, what steps would you take?

Identifying that a project is going off track is the first step in course correction. My approach to get the project back on track would include the following steps:

1. Understand the Issue: First, I would try to understand the exact problem that's causing the project to go off track. Is it due to changes in requirements, miscommunication, technical difficulties, or underestimation of resources and time? This

can be done through open communication with the team, reviewing project reports, and evaluating performance metrics.

2. Evaluate the Impact: Once I've understood the problem, I would assess the extent of the impact on the project's timeline, cost, and quality. This would give me a clearer picture of the severity of the problem and help in formulating a suitable recovery plan.

3. Create a Recovery Plan: Depending on the issues identified and their impact, I would create a plan to bring the project back on track. This could involve reallocating resources, rescheduling tasks, seeking additional funding, or refining the scope of the project.

4. Communicate with Stakeholders: Transparency is key in such situations. I would communicate the issues, the impact, and the proposed recovery plan to all stakeholders. This includes the project team, project sponsor, and any clients. Clear and honest communication can help ensure everyone understands the situation and is aligned with the recovery plan.

5. Implement the Recovery Plan: Once the plan has been agreed upon, it's time to put it into action. This could involve a range of actions, from reassigning tasks and bringing in additional resources to adjusting the project's scope or deadline.

6. Monitor Progress: After the recovery plan is implemented, it's crucial to closely monitor the project's progress to ensure

that it's moving back on track. Regular updates and check-ins will be necessary here.

For instance, during my tenure at CyanGate, we once found ourselves behind schedule on the implementation of a Product Information Management (PIM) system due to some unforeseen technical challenges. By following these steps, we managed to get the project back on track, without compromising the final deliverable's quality.

Suppose you are asked to start working on a project without clear requirements. What would be your first steps?

Starting a project without clear requirements can be a daunting task, but it's not uncommon in the dynamic world of business. In such situations, I would take the following steps:

1. Engage with Key Stakeholders: My first step would be to schedule meetings with all the key stakeholders involved in the project, including the project sponsor, end-users, and any other important decision-makers. The goal of these meetings would be to gain a better understanding of the project objectives, expectations, and the business problem the project is trying to solve.

2. Gather High-Level Requirements: Even without detailed requirements, we can often get a sense of the high-level requirements by understanding the problem that the project is trying to solve. During these initial meetings, I would attempt to define the scope of the project and gather as much information as possible about the high-level business and user requirements.

3. Identify Constraints and Assumptions: Without clear requirements, there are bound to be assumptions and constraints. I would aim to clarify these as early as possible, as they can greatly affect how the project progresses. These may include budget constraints, timeframes, technological considerations, or legal requirements.

4. Conduct Market Research: If applicable, I would also conduct some market research to understand industry standards, competitor offerings, and user expectations. This information can help us make informed decisions about the project's direction in the absence of clear requirements.

5. Formulate Initial Project Plan: Based on the information gathered, I would formulate an initial project plan including key milestones, resources, and a timeline. This plan would remain flexible, ready to adapt as we get more clarity on the requirements.

6. Iterative Requirements Gathering: As the project progresses, I would continue to refine and detail the requirements iteratively. This could involve regular meetings with stakeholders, prototyping, user interviews, and so on. This Agile approach is often the best way to handle projects where requirements are not clear at the start.

During my time at Motivity Labs, I was often faced with projects that began with ambiguous requirements. Through this approach, we were able to successfully execute the projects, gradually refining our understanding of the requirements and adjusting our plan as we progressed.

Imagine you have a colleague who is resisting change during a project. How would you handle this situation?

Resistance to change is quite common in the workplace, especially during periods of significant transformation or evolution, such as during a new project. Here's how I would handle a colleague who is resistant to change:

1. Empathize and Understand: First, I would engage in a conversation with the colleague to understand their perspective and the reasons behind their resistance. Is it because of a fear of losing control, lack of understanding of the change, or concerns about job security? By showing empathy and understanding, it can make the colleague more open to discussing their concerns.

2. Communicate the Need for Change: Once I understand their concerns, I would explain the need for the change. This could involve discussing the benefits of the change for the team, the project, and the organization as a whole. Clear and effective communication can help alleviate fears and uncertainty.

3. Involve them in the Process: If possible, I would involve the colleague in the change process. By giving them a role or responsibility in the change, it can give them a sense of ownership and control, which can make them more open to the change.

4. Provide Support and Training: If the resistance is due to a lack of knowledge or skills related to the change, I would arrange for appropriate training or support. This can help the

colleague feel more confident and competent, reducing resistance.

5. Celebrate Small Wins: Recognizing and celebrating small victories related to the change can help create a positive perception of the change. This can motivate the team and reduce resistance.

During my time at V Group Inc., we underwent a significant shift in our payment management portal project. One of our team members was resistant to the change initially. By empathizing, clearly communicating the need for the change, involving him in the process, and celebrating small wins, we were able to alleviate his concerns and gain his support for the change.

Suppose you find an error in your data analysis. What would you do?

Discovering an error in data analysis is not uncommon, but how it's addressed can have significant implications on the project and decision-making process. Here's the approach I would take:

1. Verify the Error: The first step is to confirm if the error is indeed an error. It might be a misinterpretation or a data anomaly, so it's important to go back to the data and validate the results before jumping to conclusions.

2. Understand the Root Cause: Once I've verified that there is indeed an error, I would try to understand the cause. Is it due to incorrect data, an issue with the data analysis tools, or a mistake in the calculations or methodology used?

3. Rectify the Error: After understanding the root cause, I would rectify the error. This could involve cleaning the data, correcting the calculations, or using a different method for analysis.

4. Re-Analyze the Data: After rectifying the error, I would perform the data analysis again to ensure the results are now accurate.

5. Document the Error and Resolution: I would document the error, the steps taken to resolve it, and any changes in the results or conclusions due to the error. This is important for transparency and to ensure learnings from the incident are captured for future reference.

6. Communicate: If the error impacted any decisions or reports, I would communicate the corrected analysis to all relevant stakeholders. This would involve explaining the error, the impact it had, and the steps taken to rectify it. This can help maintain trust and integrity in the data analysis process.

For example, while working at V Group Inc., I discovered an error in my analysis of the payment management portal's efficiency. After going through these steps, I found that an incorrect calculation was the cause. I corrected the error, re-analyzed the data, documented the error and resolution, and communicated the corrected results to the stakeholders. This ultimately led to more accurate insights and decisions.

How would you handle a situation where you have multiple tasks with the same deadline?

Handling multiple tasks with the same deadline can be challenging, but with a structured approach, it's manageable. Here's how I would handle it:

1. Prioritize the Tasks: The first step is to understand the importance and urgency of each task. I would assess the tasks based on their impact on the project, their dependencies, and the effort needed to complete them. Some tasks, although they have the same deadline, may need to be started earlier due to their complexity or dependencies.

2. Create a Plan: Once the tasks are prioritized, I would create a schedule or plan that outlines when and how I will complete each task. This includes breaking down larger tasks into smaller, manageable tasks and estimating the time required for each.

3. Leverage Resources: If the tasks are too much for one person to handle, I would consider delegating some tasks to other team members or seeking their assistance. It's important to leverage the skills and abilities of the team effectively.

4. Stay Organized and Focused: Keeping track of multiple tasks requires good organizational skills. I would use project management tools to keep track of my progress and stay focused.

5. Communicate: If despite all the planning and organizing, it becomes clear that all tasks can't be completed on time, it's important to communicate this as early as possible to the

relevant stakeholders. In such situations, it may be possible to negotiate extensions or re-prioritize the tasks.

6. Avoid Multitasking: Despite the common belief, multitasking can lead to lower productivity. Therefore, I would focus on one task at a time and move to the next only after the previous one is completed.

While working at Motivity Labs, there were instances when I had to handle multiple tasks with the same deadline. By prioritizing tasks, creating a clear plan, and maintaining focus, I was able to effectively manage my workload and meet the deadlines.

If you were faced with a problem that you've never encountered before, how would you approach it?

Facing new problems is a routine part of a Business Analyst's job, and it's an opportunity for learning and growth. Here's how I'd approach a problem that I've never encountered before:

1. Understand the Problem: The first step is to thoroughly understand the problem. I'd ask probing questions, review relevant documentation, and speak with key stakeholders to get a complete picture of the issue.

2. Research: If it's a problem I've never encountered before, I'd conduct research to understand if others have faced similar issues and how they resolved it. This could involve online research, reviewing industry case studies, or speaking with colleagues or peers in the industry.

3. Identify Potential Solutions: Based on my understanding of the problem and the research, I'd brainstorm and identify potential solutions. I'd also seek input from others to get a diversity of ideas.

4. Evaluate Solutions: Once potential solutions are identified, I'd evaluate them based on their feasibility, impact, cost, time required, and alignment with the business objectives.

5. Choose and Implement Solution: I'd choose the solution that best fits the situation and implement it, keeping stakeholders informed about the process and setting realistic expectations.

6. Monitor and Adjust: After implementation, I'd monitor the results closely to ensure the solution is effective. If it's not working as expected, I'd be prepared to make adjustments or try a different solution.

7. Document and Share Learnings: I believe it's important to document new problems and their solutions for future reference. I'd also share my learnings with my team to contribute to our collective knowledge base.

For instance, during my tenure at CyanGate, I faced a new challenge while enabling the Product Information Management (PIM) system for auto-tagging. Through thorough understanding, diligent research, and collaborative brainstorming, we were able to devise and implement a solution that significantly improved retail workflows.

Imagine you are unable to meet a project deadline due to an unforeseen issue. How would you communicate this to stakeholders?

Communicating delays or issues with a project is never an easy task, but it's crucial for maintaining transparency and trust with stakeholders. Here's how I would approach it:

1. Understand the Issue: First, I would thoroughly understand the unforeseen issue that caused the delay. It's important to know the cause, its impact on the project timeline, and the proposed solution or plan to resolve it.

2. Develop a Contingency Plan: Before communicating the issue to the stakeholders, I would develop a contingency plan to address the delay. This plan would include a revised project timeline, additional resources if necessary, and the steps to prevent such issues in the future.

3. Communicate Early and Honestly: As soon as I understand the impact of the issue on the project timeline, I would communicate the situation to the stakeholders. Transparency is key - I would explain the issue, its impact on the project, and the steps we're taking to mitigate it.

4. Use the Right Medium: Depending on the severity of the delay and the stakeholders involved, I might choose to communicate this information via email or set up a meeting to discuss the issue in person. The goal is to make sure all stakeholders fully understand the situation and have an opportunity to ask questions or provide input.

5. Apologize and Reassure: I would apologize for the delay and reassure the stakeholders that the team is working diligently to resolve the issue and get the project back on track.

6. Follow-up: After the initial communication, I would provide regular updates to keep the stakeholders informed about the progress in resolving the issue and any changes to the revised timeline.

For example, when I was working at V Group Inc, we encountered an unforeseen issue while implementing a new payment management portal that caused a delay in the project. I communicated this to our stakeholders as soon as we understood the problem, provided regular updates, and was able to successfully manage their expectations while we resolved the issue.

5. **Role-specific Questions**: These questions focus on your understanding of the business analyst role and related responsibilities.

What is your process for gathering and documenting business requirements?

Gathering and documenting business requirements is a crucial part of a business analyst's role. Here is the process I typically follow:

1. Understand the Business Context: Before starting the requirement gathering process, I first aim to understand the business context, including the objectives, challenges, and the

key stakeholders. This gives me a clearer idea of what we are trying to achieve.

2. Identify Stakeholders: Identifying all relevant stakeholders is crucial. These can include business users, project sponsors, subject matter experts, and IT personnel. Each stakeholder may have unique insights and requirements for the project.

3. Plan the Requirement Gathering Process: Depending on the project, stakeholders, and complexity, I decide on the best methods to gather requirements. These can include interviews, workshops, surveys, document analysis, and observing business processes.

4. Conduct Requirement Gathering Sessions: I organize and conduct the requirement gathering sessions using the identified methods. Here, active listening and asking the right questions is key to ensure all important details are captured.

5. Document the Requirements: I ensure that all gathered requirements are documented clearly and in detail. This usually involves creating a Business Requirement Document (BRD) which outlines what the business needs from the project. This document typically includes the project scope, business and user requirements, any identified constraints, and acceptance criteria.

6. Validate and Confirm Requirements: Once the BRD is created, I review it with the stakeholders to confirm that the documented requirements accurately reflect their needs and expectations. This step helps to ensure that there are no misunderstandings or gaps in the requirements.

7. Manage and Maintain Requirements: Post-validation, requirements may evolve or change during the project life cycle. I ensure to manage these changes and maintain the documentation, ensuring it is always up-to-date.

For instance, while at V Group Inc., I led the requirements gathering process for a new payment management portal. I conducted multiple stakeholder interviews, facilitated workshops, and used my analytical skills to translate these business needs into detailed functional specifications. These efforts ensured we had a clear, agreed-upon direction for the project, resulting in a successful implementation.

How would you conduct a feasibility study for a new project?

Conducting a feasibility study is crucial to assess if a project is viable and worth pursuing. Here are the steps I follow when conducting a feasibility study:

1. Define the Scope of the Project: Clearly defining the project scope is the first step in a feasibility study. It includes understanding the project's goals, the problems it intends to solve, the target audience, and the key deliverables.

2. Market Analysis: If the project involves introducing a new product or service, I conduct a market analysis. This involves understanding the target market, customer needs, and the competitive landscape.

3. Technical Feasibility: I assess if we have the necessary technology and infrastructure to implement the project. This involves understanding the technical requirements,

identifying potential technical challenges, and assessing how these can be addressed.

4. Economic Feasibility: This involves assessing the financial implications of the project. I'd consider the project's costs (both initial and ongoing), potential revenue, and return on investment. A cost-benefit analysis is often useful in this stage.

5. Operational Feasibility: I determine if the project can be integrated into the existing operational processes. This includes considering the impact on the current workflow, the ease of use for the end-users, and how much training would be required.

6. Legal and Regulatory Feasibility: This involves assessing whether the project complies with all relevant laws and regulations.

7. Schedule Feasibility: I analyze if the project can be completed within the desired timeframe considering the resources and constraints.

8. Risk Assessment: I identify potential risks and uncertainties associated with the project and develop strategies to mitigate them.

9. Prepare the Feasibility Report: Finally, I compile all the information into a feasibility report, summarizing the findings and making a recommendation on whether to proceed with the project.

For example, while at Motivity Labs Inc., I was involved in conducting a feasibility study for an automated financing model. By thoroughly analyzing technical, economic, operational, and scheduling feasibilities, we were able to make an informed decision to proceed with the project, which ultimately proved to be successful.

Can you explain how a Business Analyst fits into the project management process?

The roles of a Business Analyst (BA) and a Project Manager (PM) can be quite interconnected, and a BA plays a crucial role in the project management process.

1. Initiation Phase: In the initiation phase of a project, the BA usually helps to define the project's scope and objectives. This involves identifying the business problem or opportunity, conducting a preliminary analysis, and contributing to the business case that justifies the initiation of the project.

2. Planning Phase: During the planning phase, the BA works closely with the PM to identify stakeholders, establish project requirements, and help devise a detailed project plan. They may also assist in preparing the project's risk management plan by identifying potential risks and mitigation strategies.

3. Execution Phase: In the execution phase, the BA often serves as a liaison between the project team and stakeholders. They translate business requirements into functional specifications, work with the team to ensure they understand what needs to be done, and help validate the solutions. They may also assist with change management and help to manage stakeholder expectations.

4. Monitoring and Controlling Phase: BAs play a critical role in monitoring and controlling the project's progress. They ensure the solution being developed aligns with the business requirements, validate changes, and assist with user acceptance testing. They also help to track and manage changes to the project scope.

5. Closing Phase: Once the project is ready for delivery, the BA helps to ensure that the solution meets business needs and can help with training and documentation. After the project's completion, they may also be involved in post-implementation review processes to identify lessons learned and improve future projects.

In essence, a Business Analyst's role in project management is to ensure that the project's output aligns with the business needs and adds value to the organization. It's about ensuring that the 'what' (the requirements and business needs defined by the BA) aligns with the 'how' (the project management and execution led by the PM).

How do you identify risks and issues during a project?

Identifying risks and issues during a project is a critical part of a business analyst's role and can often make the difference between a successful project and one that encounters significant difficulties. Here are the steps I typically follow:

1. Understand the Project Scope and Context: To begin, it's crucial to have a thorough understanding of the project's goals, scope, and context. This knowledge forms the basis for identifying potential risks and issues that could arise.

273

2. Conduct Risk Identification Workshops: I organize workshops with stakeholders, project team members, and subject matter experts to brainstorm potential risks and issues. These collaborative sessions can be incredibly effective in unearthing risks that might not be immediately obvious.

3. Review Project Documentation: By studying all project documents - such as the project charter, business requirements document, project plan, etc., - I can often identify areas of uncertainty or ambiguity that may present risks.

4. Leverage Past Experiences: Reviewing past projects or talking to colleagues who have worked on similar projects can provide valuable insights into potential risks and issues.

5. Ongoing Risk and Issue Identification: Risk and issue identification is not a one-time activity. As the project progresses, new risks and issues may emerge, so I make sure to keep this as an ongoing activity throughout the project.

6. Utilize Risk Identification Tools and Techniques: There are several risk identification tools and techniques like SWOT analysis, PESTLE analysis, and Failure Mode and Effects Analysis (FMEA) that can help in identifying potential risks and issues.

Once identified, each risk or issue is logged in a risk or issue register, where it is evaluated, prioritized based on its potential impact and likelihood of occurrence, and assigned an owner. A mitigation or response strategy is then developed for each risk.

For instance, while at V Group Inc., during the implementation of a payment management portal, we identified the risk of potential data breaches. We prioritized this risk due to its high impact and took proactive measures, like incorporating advanced encryption and security practices, to mitigate it effectively.

How do you manage change requests from stakeholders?

Managing change requests is an integral part of a business analyst's role. Here's my usual approach:

1. Log the Request: The first step when a change request comes in is to log it in a designated change request log or system. This involves recording essential details such as who made the request, what the change entails, and why it was proposed.

2. Evaluate the Request: Next, I work with relevant stakeholders, including the project team, to evaluate the change request. This evaluation often includes understanding the impact of the change on the project's timeline, cost, resources, and whether it aligns with the project's scope and objectives.

3. Analyze the Impact: A crucial part of evaluating the change request is conducting an impact analysis. This involves identifying all the areas that will be affected by the change and estimating the effort required to implement it.

4. Discuss with Stakeholders: Once the impact analysis is done, I discuss the findings with the necessary stakeholders. These discussions often include presenting the pros and cons,

the impact on the project, and potential alternatives, if applicable.

5. Get Approval: If the stakeholders agree that the change is necessary, the request is then presented to the Change Control Board (CCB) or a similar authority for approval. The CCB's role is to assess the change from a broader organizational perspective and approve, reject, or request more information.

6. Implement the Change: If the change is approved, the project plan is updated, and the project team is informed. The change is then implemented, and its progress is closely tracked and managed.

7. Document the Change: Finally, it's crucial to document all changes thoroughly, including their impact and how they were managed. This documentation aids future projects and serves as a record of why certain decisions were made.

For example, while I was working at V Group Inc., we received a request to add a new feature to the payment management portal we were developing. I led the evaluation of the request, conducted an impact analysis, discussed it with the stakeholders, and took it to the CCB. Upon approval, I worked with the project team to implement the change, ensuring the project still delivered on time and within budget.

What techniques do you use to ensure that you understand the client's needs?

Understanding a client's needs is fundamental to the role of a business analyst. There are several techniques I use to ensure I accurately capture and understand these needs:

1. Stakeholder Interviews: One-on-one interviews with key stakeholders are an excellent way to gather detailed insights about their expectations, requirements, and potential challenges. It's a direct and interactive way to understand what they need from the project.

2. Workshops or Focus Groups: Organizing workshops or focus groups with different stakeholders allows me to facilitate discussions and gather diverse perspectives. This method can often help uncover requirements that weren't initially obvious.

3. Surveys and Questionnaires: These are useful when there are many stakeholders, and it's not feasible to interview or conduct workshops with all of them. Surveys and questionnaires can be used to gather broad insights, which can then be followed up with interviews for more depth.

4. Document Analysis: Reviewing existing documentation, such as strategy documents, current process guides, and system specifications, can provide valuable context and help me understand the current state and what needs to change.

5. Observation or Job Shadowing: Directly observing stakeholders as they perform their duties can provide firsthand insights into how things are done, the challenges faced, and the improvements needed.

6. Prototypes and Use Cases: Developing prototypes or use cases can help stakeholders visualize the proposed solution, clarify their needs, and provide feedback.

7. User Stories: In Agile environments, I work with stakeholders to develop user stories, which are a simple and effective way to capture requirements from the end-user perspective.

For example, while working at Motivity Labs, I was assigned to develop an automated financing model for a consumer finance company. I conducted a series of stakeholder interviews and workshops to understand their needs better, which helped us deliver a solution that met their expectations and requirements.

Can you describe your experience with User Acceptance Testing (UAT)?

User Acceptance Testing (UAT) has been a significant part of my roles as a business analyst across various projects

UAT is the final stage of testing, where end-users test the system to verify if it meets their requirements and is ready for delivery. My responsibility typically begins with the development of a UAT plan, which outlines the testing strategy, schedule, resources required, and specific test cases.

I usually create test scenarios and test cases based on the requirements and functionality of the system. These test cases are designed to cover all the possible user interactions with the system, including edge cases, and are documented and reviewed by stakeholders before testing begins.

During the testing phase, I act as a facilitator, coordinating between the users performing the testing and the development team. This coordination involves helping users understand the testing process, troubleshooting any issues they encounter, and tracking the progress of testing.

When users identify issues or bugs, I help document them, prioritize based on their severity, and communicate them to the development team for fixes. After the issues are resolved, I ensure that the fixes are retested and confirmed by the users.

At my role at Motivity Labs Inc, I was actively involved in the UAT phase of the automated financing model project. I developed test scenarios, coordinated the testing process, and acted as a liaison between the end-users and the development team. This experience provided me with a deep understanding of the UAT process, which has been invaluable in subsequent roles.

Overall, my experience with UAT has taught me that effective communication, careful planning, and close collaboration with all parties involved are key to a successful UAT process.

How do you ensure effective communication between different project teams?

Effective communication between different project teams is crucial for the success of any project. I employ several strategies to ensure smooth and efficient communication:

1. Establish Clear Channels of Communication: One of the first things I do is set up defined channels for different types of communication. This could be emails for formal

communication, instant messaging platforms for quick queries, and regular meetings or calls for in-depth discussions.

2. Regular Meetings: I ensure that there are regular meetings between teams, including stand-ups, progress meetings, and retrospective meetings. In an Agile environment, daily scrum meetings are a great way to keep everyone updated about what each team member is working on and any challenges they are facing.

3. Stakeholder Maps: Understanding who needs what information is crucial. I create stakeholder maps to understand everyone's roles, responsibilities, and information needs, which helps in directing the right information to the right people at the right time.

4. Project Management Tools: Using project management tools can help track the progress of tasks, manage dependencies between teams, and provide visibility to all stakeholders. Tools like JIRA, Trello, or Asana can be very useful in this regard.

5. Transparency and Openness: I encourage an environment where everyone feels comfortable asking questions, sharing ideas, and raising concerns. This helps prevent misunderstandings and ensures that everyone has the information they need.

6. Documentation: I ensure all crucial decisions, changes, and updates are documented and shared with all relevant parties. This can act as a reference and avoid confusion.

7. Active Listening and Feedback: Communication is not just about speaking; it's also about listening. I ensure that I listen to the teams' input and feedback actively and make adjustments as needed.

For instance, in my previous role at V Group Inc., we had teams spread across different geographies, so effective communication was key. I set up regular meetings across different time zones, used project management tools for visibility, and ensured that all important decisions and changes were well-documented and communicated promptly to all stakeholders. This approach helped in maintaining effective communication between the teams and led to successful project outcomes.

Can you explain the concept of business process improvement?

Business process improvement (BPI) is a strategic planning methodology aimed at identifying the operations or employee skills that could be improved to boost productivity, efficiency, and effectiveness in an organization. It is a key responsibility of business analysts, and I have had considerable experience with it in my previous roles.

BPI involves the following steps:

1. Identifying Current Processes: First, you need to understand and document the current business processes. This could be done through various methods, such as observing workflows, conducting interviews, or reviewing documentation.

2. Analyzing the Process: Once you have a clear understanding of the process, you analyze it to identify any bottlenecks, inefficiencies, or areas for potential improvement. This analysis can be done using various techniques such as data analysis, process modelling, or root cause analysis.

3. Envisioning the Future Process: Based on the insights from the analysis, you propose an improved process that addresses the identified issues. This could involve restructuring workflows, automating tasks, implementing new technologies, or improving communication channels.

4. Implementing the Changes: The proposed changes are then implemented. This could involve change management processes to ensure that employees understand and accept the changes, training sessions to teach employees any new skills required, and potentially pilot programs to test the new process.

5. Review and Continual Improvement: After the changes are implemented, it's crucial to review the new process to ensure it's working as intended and delivering the expected benefits. This involves monitoring key performance indicators (KPIs), soliciting feedback from employees, and making any necessary adjustments.

In my previous role at V Group Inc., I successfully applied BPI to the implementation of a new payment management portal. After carefully analyzing the existing payment process, we identified several areas for improvement, such as streamlining the payment approval process and automating certain manual tasks. The implementation of these improvements led to a more efficient process, increased data accuracy, and improved customer relationship management.

What steps do you take to ensure that a project's scope is well-defined?

Defining the project's scope is an essential part of project planning and management, and it involves clearly outlining what the project will achieve, what work will be done, and the boundaries of the project. Here are the steps I take to ensure a project's scope is well-defined:

1. Understanding Stakeholder Needs: The first step is to understand what the stakeholders want from the project. This can be done through interviews, workshops, or surveys. I make sure to interact with all the stakeholders, including customers, project team members, management, and end-users, to understand their needs, expectations, and constraints.

2. Defining Goals and Objectives: After understanding the needs of the stakeholders, I help in defining clear, measurable, and achievable goals and objectives for the project. These should align with the strategic objectives of the organization and satisfy the needs of the stakeholders.

3. Identifying Deliverables: These are the tangible outcomes or results of the project. They could be products, services, or improvements in processes. Each deliverable is described in detail including its specifications, characteristics, and requirements.

4. Determining Scope Boundaries: It's crucial to define what's in scope and what's out of scope. This helps in setting clear boundaries for the project and prevents scope creep, where the project's scope gradually expands beyond its original objectives.

5. Creating the Work Breakdown Structure (WBS): The WBS is a hierarchical decomposition of the project into manageable chunks or work packages. It helps in understanding all the tasks that need to be performed to create the deliverables.

6. Documenting the Project Scope: Once the above steps are completed, everything is documented in a project scope statement. This document serves as a reference for everyone involved in the project and helps ensure everyone has a shared understanding of the project's scope.

7. Getting Approval: The project scope statement is reviewed by the stakeholders and approved. This approval ensures that everyone agrees on the project's scope before work begins.

8. Managing and Controlling Scope: Throughout the project, the scope should be monitored and controlled to prevent scope creep. Any changes to the scope should go through a formal change control process.

In my role at V Group Inc., I was involved in defining the scope for the implementation of a new payment management portal. We used a structured approach similar to the one I described, which helped us in managing the project effectively and delivering it successfully.

6. **Domain-specific Questions**: If the business analyst role is related to a specific industry (like healthcare, finance, IT, etc.), you may be asked questions relevant to that domain.

IT Domain as an Example:

Can you explain how you've incorporated IT solutions into business strategies in the past?

During my tenure at V Group Inc., we implemented a payment management portal for a law firm. This project involved careful integration of IT solutions into a broader business strategy. The goal was to streamline the payment process, making it more efficient for the end-users.

After conducting a thorough analysis of the existing business processes and identifying areas for improvement, we recommended the creation of a digital payment system. I played a key role in gathering requirements and collaborating with cross-functional teams to align these requirements with the business goals. I also acted as the liaison between business stakeholders and our offshore IT teams to translate these business requirements into technical specifications.

The result was the creation of a new payment system called "Self Pay". It significantly improved the firm's operational efficiency and led to increased customer satisfaction. By incorporating this IT solution into the business strategy, we not only streamlined the payment process but also significantly improved the overall customer experience.

How have you used technology to improve business processes?

I've had a few opportunities where I used technology to improve business processes.

One example that comes to mind is from my time with CyanGate, where I worked on improving retail workflows through the enablement of a Product Information Management (PIM) system for Auto-Tagging. This technology enhancement resulted in more efficient product categorization and improved the quality of product data, which ultimately led to a more seamless shopping experience for customers.

Another notable example was during my tenure at V Group Inc. Here, I was part of the team that implemented a new payment system called "Self Pay". This digital payment system streamlined the end-user payment process for a law firm, improved data accuracy, and enhanced the efficiency of customer relationship management.

In both instances, the use of technology allowed us to improve the quality, efficiency, and effectiveness of business operations. By automating manual processes and using data more effectively, we were able to deliver better outcomes for the business and its customers.

How would you handle a situation where the IT solution you proposed was not accepted by the business stakeholders?

In my experience as a Business Analyst, I've learned that not every solution proposed will be accepted by business stakeholders, and that's okay. It's part of the process. Here's how I would handle a situation where a proposed IT solution was not accepted:

1. Understand Their Concerns: First, I would seek to understand the reasons behind their decision. I'd ask for detailed feedback on why the solution was not accepted. It could be due to budget constraints, timeline, complexities, lack of alignment with business goals, or they might foresee risks or challenges that I may not have considered.

2. Reevaluate the Proposal: Based on their feedback, I would reevaluate the proposed solution. I'd analyze whether there are modifications or alternative solutions that could address their concerns and still meet the project goals.

3. Communicate and Collaborate: I would then communicate these modifications or propose alternative solutions to the stakeholders. It's crucial to involve them in the decision-making process and ensure they feel their concerns are addressed.

4. Re-Present the Solution: After making necessary changes and ensuring alignment with stakeholder needs and project goals, I would re-present the solution to the stakeholders for approval. I would clearly articulate how this revised solution addresses their concerns and meets the project objectives.

5. Escalation: If the revised solution is still not accepted, and I firmly believe it's the right course of action, I would consider escalating the issue to higher management or a project sponsor, providing them with a comprehensive understanding of the situation and potential impacts.

6. Acceptance and Moving Forward: If all efforts fail, it's important to remember that ultimate decision-making often rests with the business stakeholders. I would respect their decision, learn from the experience, and move forward, focusing on finding a new, acceptable solution.

In my previous role at Motivity Labs, we were proposing an automated finance model. Initially, it was met with resistance due to apprehensions about the transition from traditional methods. By actively listening, addressing concerns, and showcasing potential benefits, we were able to gain stakeholder buy-in and successfully implement the system.

What is your experience with cloud computing and its implementation in business processes?

Throughout my career as a Business Analyst, I've been part of several projects that leveraged cloud computing technology to improve business processes. I'm not a cloud computing engineer, but my role as a business analyst often involves understanding the potential of technologies like cloud computing and facilitating their use to improve business outcomes.

While at V Group Inc., I worked on a significant project involving the implementation of a payment management portal for facilitating end-user payments for a law firm. The system we implemented was cloud-based, and this brought several advantages, such as flexibility, scalability, and cost-efficiency. My role was to understand the business requirements, translate them into functional specifications, and communicate these to the offshore IT teams. I also assisted in creating detailed requirement documents and use cases for this cloud-based system.

At Motivity Labs Inc., I worked on an automated financing model based on technology-driven business processes. Again, this was a cloud-based system, and my role included gathering requirements, conducting gap analysis for process improvement initiatives, and assisting in managing the project.

Cloud computing brings a lot of benefits to businesses, including easy access to data, cost savings by eliminating the need for in-house server storage and application requirements, automatic software integration, and quick scalability. It also offers the potential for collaboration efficiency, allowing globally dispersed teams to collaborate on projects more efficiently.

Understanding how to utilize cloud-based solutions to meet business objectives is a crucial part of my role as a business analyst. The cloud is the future of technology in business, and I'm excited to be a part of projects that leverage this technology to drive business growth and efficiency.

Can you discuss a time when you were responsible for implementing a new software system?

One prominent instance of implementing a new software system was during my tenure at V Group Inc. where I played a crucial role in the implementation of a payment management portal for a law firm. The aim was to facilitate end-user payments, thus improving the overall efficiency of their payment process.

During the initial phase of the project, I was responsible for conducting a thorough analysis of the business processes to understand the current system and identify areas for improvement. This required close collaboration with cross-functional teams to gather requirements and elicit stakeholder feedback to ensure alignment with business goals and objectives.

Based on the gathered information, I created detailed requirement documents, use cases, and functional specifications. This helped in bridging the gap between the business needs and the technical capabilities of the new software system. I worked closely with the technical team to ensure that they had a clear understanding of these requirements.

Throughout the project, I acted as a liaison between the business stakeholders and offshore IT teams, translating business requirements into technical specifications, and ensuring that both sides were on the same page.

Once the development phase was complete, I was also involved in coordinating user acceptance testing, ensuring that the implemented system met the defined business requirements. After successful testing, I assisted in the rollout and post-implementation support.

The project was a success and led to improved data accuracy and increased efficiency in customer relationship management. It also resulted in an enhanced user experience due to the simplified and streamlined payment process.

This experience gave me an in-depth understanding of the challenges and intricacies involved in software implementation projects and helped me develop effective strategies to handle similar projects in the future.

What experience do you have with data privacy and security?

Data privacy and security have been integral aspects of my role as a Business Analyst, especially given the increasing reliance on digital systems and data-driven decision making in today's business landscape.

While I was working at V Group Inc., one of my projects involved the implementation of a payment management portal for a law firm. Given the sensitive nature of the data being processed, ensuring data privacy and security was a top priority. My responsibilities included ensuring that our requirements documents and functional specifications clearly defined the data privacy and security requirements. I worked closely with the technical teams to ensure that they understood and adhered to these requirements during development. Furthermore, I was involved in the testing process, where we thoroughly tested the system to ensure these data privacy and security requirements were met.

In addition to this, at Motivity Labs, I was involved in a project implementing an automated financing model for a consumer finance company. Again, considering the highly sensitive financial data involved, stringent data privacy and security measures were of utmost importance.

Furthermore, I always stay updated with the latest data protection regulations and industry standards, such as GDPR and ISO 27001, to ensure that the solutions we provide are compliant with these regulations.

Though not directly in charge of implementing security measures – as it's typically the role of IT and security teams, I see my role as a Business Analyst as being a facilitator and advocate for data privacy and security, ensuring these critical elements are accounted for during the planning, requirements gathering, and implementation stages of a project.

Can you explain your understanding of IT service management?

IT Service Management, or ITSM, is a strategic approach directed towards the design, delivery, management, and improvement of the way information technology is used within an organization. The fundamental goal of ITSM is to ensure that the right processes, people, and technology are in place so that the organization can meet its business goals.

ITSM is not just about the IT team managing the IT systems, but also about how IT interacts with business customers and users, and how IT strategy aligns with business objectives. It's about delivering IT as a service, where the focus is on customer needs, customer outcomes, and a value-based approach.

Various frameworks and standards can guide ITSM practices, with ITIL (Information Technology Infrastructure Library) being one of the most widely used. ITIL provides a set of best practices that focus on aligning IT services with the needs of the business. Other frameworks include COBIT, which provides an overall governance and control framework, and ISO/IEC 20000, which is the international standard for IT service management.

As a Business Analyst, my role often intersects with ITSM when it comes to understanding the business needs and translating them into IT requirements. In many projects, I have collaborated closely with IT service management teams to ensure that the implemented IT solutions align with the strategic goals of the organization, are delivered efficiently, and bring value to the business.

In essence, effective ITSM is a key component of any successful business that relies heavily on technology to deliver its products or services. Understanding the principles of ITSM enables a Business Analyst like myself to contribute more effectively to the organization's success.

What is your experience with data migration projects?

In my capacity as a Business Analyst, I have been involved in several data migration projects. My role in such projects typically includes understanding the business requirements, defining the data migration strategy, facilitating communication between business stakeholders and technical teams, and validating the results of the data migration.

One particular project that comes to mind was during my time at Motivity Labs Inc. We were tasked with developing an automated financing model for a consumer finance company which required the migration of a large volume of financial data from legacy systems to a new platform. This data was crucial for forecasting and analysis purposes.

The data migration process was multifaceted, and it involved several steps:

1. Data Assessment: We initially identified what data needed to be moved to the new platform. This involved closely working with business stakeholders and understanding their data needs.

2. Mapping: Once we had a clear understanding of the data required, we mapped the source data to the target data fields in the new system.

3. Data Cleaning: Prior to migration, we had to ensure the data was clean and accurate. This involved identifying any inconsistencies or discrepancies in the legacy system data and resolving them before migration.

4. Migration and Validation: The cleaned data was then migrated to the new system, after which we conducted thorough testing to ensure the data was accurately transferred and that the new system was functioning as expected.

5. User Training: After successful data migration, I was also involved in training end-users to adapt to the new system and understand how to use the migrated data effectively.

The project was successful, largely due to the collaborative efforts of the entire team and the rigorous processes we followed. The new automated financing model greatly improved the client's ability to make data-driven decisions, thereby increasing their operational efficiency.

These experiences have given me a solid foundation in handling data migration projects, and I understand the complexities and challenges that such projects can entail. It's a critical process that, when done right, can lead to significant business benefits.

Can you discuss any IT risk assessment methods you've used in the past?

Risk assessment is a key part of any project, and in the IT sector, it's crucial for identifying potential issues that could impact the delivery or performance of a system or application. In my role as a Business Analyst, I've been involved in risk assessments using various methods.

One commonly used method is the qualitative risk assessment. This involves identifying potential risks, assigning them a likelihood of occurrence based on historical data or expert opinion, and then determining the potential impact on the project if the risk were to materialize. The risk is then rated based on its likelihood and impact, which helps prioritize the mitigation strategies.

In one of my projects at CyanGate, LLC, we were implementing a Product Information Management (PIM) system for Auto-Tagging. We conducted a qualitative risk assessment where we identified potential risks such as potential delays in data migration, technical issues with the PIM system, and resistance to change from end-users. Each risk was rated based on its potential impact and likelihood of occurrence. This helped us develop a risk mitigation plan that included regular progress tracking, technical troubleshooting, and end-user training, which ensured the successful implementation of the system.

Another method I've utilized is a quantitative risk assessment. This involves a numerical or measurable value attached to the likelihood of the risk and its impact. This method is useful when dealing with financial risks or when a more precise assessment is required. However, it often requires more data and can be more complex to perform.

Apart from these, I also believe in the importance of continual risk monitoring and reassessment throughout a project. Risks are not static and can change as the project progresses. Regular risk reviews can ensure that new risks are identified and managed appropriately, and that mitigation strategies for existing risks are working effectively.

Overall, risk assessment is about understanding what could go wrong, how likely it is, what the potential impact could be, and then deciding what actions to take to prevent or minimize the risk. As a Business Analyst, it's my responsibility to ensure that these assessments are carried out and that their outcomes are communicated to all relevant stakeholders.

What do you consider the most challenging aspect of integrating IT systems within business operations?

Integrating IT systems within business operations can be complex and challenging due to several factors:

1. User Adoption and Change Management: One of the biggest challenges is getting users to adopt new technology and adapt to changes in their workflows. People are often resistant to change, particularly if they're used to doing things a certain way and the new system disrupts that. In my experience at CyanGate, LLC, I found that effective communication, training, and a gradual rollout strategy helped to ease the transition.

2. Interoperability and Compatibility Issues: Ensuring the new IT system integrates well with the existing software and hardware is critical. If there are compatibility issues, it can lead to operational disruptions, data inaccuracies, or even system failures. It's important to conduct thorough system and integration testing to identify and fix any interoperability issues.

3. Data Migration and Security: Migrating existing data to a new system is another challenge. It's crucial to ensure that all relevant data is moved over without any loss or corruption. Moreover, ensuring the security and privacy of the data during and after the transition is paramount to maintain trust and comply with regulations.

4. Technical Challenges and System Performance: New IT systems may face technical issues, bugs, or may not perform

as expected. Continuous monitoring, testing, and tweaking are necessary to ensure optimal performance.

5. Cost and Time Constraints: IT integrations can be costly and time-consuming. Budget overruns and delays are not uncommon, which can impact the overall project success.

All of these challenges require careful planning, effective communication, strong technical expertise, and meticulous execution. As a Business Analyst, I have experienced these challenges first-hand, and I believe that with the right strategies and a proactive approach, they can be successfully managed.

Real Life Interview and answers of an ambitious Graduate Business Analyst

For this interview we would consider the below Sample Job Description:

Diligenta Job Description for Graduate Trainee – Business Analysis

Reports to: Function-specific manager, depending on placement in the Change Transformation Department, located in either Bristol or Peterborough.

Broadband/Level/Grade: TM, **Regulatory Requirements:** None.

Job Purpose: The role of the Graduate Trainee in Business Analysis at Diligenta aims to learn, assist, and perform various Change-related activities. The incumbent will be responsible for developing skills in project management, business analysis, programme office management, and test management to become employable in an established role within the Change function. This role supports the business strategy and objectives of the company.

Key Result Areas: The Graduate Trainee will be responsible for developing competence in Business Analysis and assisting in Change and Transformation activities to meet client demands. The role includes understanding different delivery lifecycles and the aspects of the Diligenta Change function. The trainee will contribute to the development and implementation of projects, take ownership of assigned tasks, understand Diligenta's position within the Financial Services outsourcing market, and communicate effectively with colleagues and stakeholders. This position also requires the development of a detailed understanding of the financial services regulated environment, effective stakeholder management skills, and the undertaking of training opportunities to consolidate skills and knowledge.

Skills and Experience:

- **Essential Qualifications:** Degree or equivalent, class 2:2 or higher, obtained in the last three years and in any discipline.

- **Essential Skills:** Numeracy, high levels of accuracy and attention to detail, IT literacy, strong communication and interpersonal skills, ability to work under pressure, ability to work in a team and independently.

- **Desirable Qualifications:** Degree in a business-related discipline.

- **Desirable Experience:** Recent work experience in a large organization or in financial services.

Dimensions Impacted By Job: The position does not manage others and does not have direct capital or revenue budgets.

Competencies: The role requires the selection of 4-6 key competencies from a given list, as well as any required technical competencies not already described in the skills section.

Interview Questions with Sample Answers:

1. Can you briefly run us through your CV?

My name is Emily Thompson, and I've built a diverse and dynamic career at the intersection of business management and data analytics.

My educational background includes a BA in Business & Management from the University of West England, a Google Data Analytics Professional Certificate from Coursera, and a Diploma in Leadership & Management from the City, University of London, among others.

I have a set of well-developed IT skills, including proficiency in SQL, Tableau, Power BI, and advanced Excel. These technical skills have enabled me to contribute effectively to various data analysis and visualisation projects. For instance, I created a global heatmap to show Covid-19 cases using Tableau, and carried out an exploratory data analysis project on the world's happiest countries using SQL & Excel.

In terms of professional experience, I have spent significant time in managerial roles. At the Entain Group, I worked as a Customer Service Manager, improving shop rating standards, expanding the customer base, and using Power BI to track and measure performance. In the hospitality sector, I worked as a Bar Manager at Chai Ki and as a Bar Supervisor at Roka Restaurant, where I implemented career development plans, fostered productive relationships, and managed bar duties for seamless operations.

As a multilingual individual with proficiency in English, Spanish, and Catalan, I've been able to communicate effectively in diverse environments, which I believe is an asset in today's globalised business world.

I'm now looking forward to leveraging my skills and experiences as a Graduate Trainee – Business Analyst at Diligenta, where I hope to contribute to change and transformation activities and develop a deep understanding of the financial services regulated environment.

2. **Can you please describe how you did Data Visualisation Project where you Created a Global heatmap to show Covid-19 cases in Tableau?**

In the data visualization project, my primary objective was to create a global heatmap to show Covid-19 cases. I started by sourcing data from a reliable public health database, which provided daily updates of Covid-19 cases across the world.

I used a CSV file, which had country-wise daily numbers of confirmed cases, deaths, and recoveries. The dataset also included geographic coordinates, which I could use to map the data. I imported this file into Tableau.

Firstly, I pre-processed the data by cleaning and formatting it into a form suitable for Tableau. I ensured that there were no missing or inconsistent entries, especially in the geographic data.

Once the data was ready, I used Tableau's inbuilt geographical plotting features to map the data onto a global map. I used the number of confirmed cases as the metric for the heatmap, with regions experiencing more cases showing up in a darker shade.

I also made the visualization interactive, allowing users to select a specific date to see the global state of Covid-19 cases at that point. This required the creation of a dynamic filter linked to the date field in the dataset.

Lastly, I added a legend to the heatmap for easy interpretation and added annotations to highlight significant data points.

This project gave me the opportunity to delve deeper into Tableau's advanced features and understand the power of effective data visualization in communicating complex data insights effectively. It was quite challenging to ensure that the data was accurately represented, and the map was easy to understand, but the end result was highly appreciated by my peers and tutors.

3. What is your understanding of Diligenta.

Diligenta is a company offering business process services for the life and pensions industry in the United Kingdom. Diligenta is a subsidiary of Tata Consultancy Services (TCS), one of the largest IT services and consulting companies globally.

Diligenta provides end-to-end policy administration services for life and pensions companies, which includes activities like claims processing, policy servicing, finance and actuarial support, among others. The company aims to streamline and digitise processes for its clients, improving efficiency, reducing costs, and enhancing customer experiences.

Diligenta has expertise in managing migrations and transformations in the life and pensions space and is known for its robust risk management and regulatory compliance practices. Given the rapidly changing regulatory landscape and increased demand for digital experiences in the financial services industry, Diligenta's services are crucial for life and pensions companies.

4. **Could you explain how you would use SQL to find the second highest salary from a table named 'Employee' with the fields 'Employee_ID' and 'Salary'? What SQL command or commands would you use and why?**

To find the second highest salary in an 'Employee' table, you could use SQL's subquery and the 'LIMIT' and 'ORDER BY' clauses.

SELECT MAX(Salary)

FROM Employee

WHERE Salary NOT IN

  (SELECT MAX(Salary)

  FROM Employee);

In this query, the subquery `(SELECT MAX(Salary) FROM Employee)` finds the maximum salary. Then, the main query finds the maximum salary among the remaining salaries (i.e., it finds the second highest salary).

Another approach that works well specifically in MySQL is using 'LIMIT' and 'ORDER BY':

SELECT Salary

FROM Employee

ORDER BY Salary DESC

LIMIT 1 OFFSET 1;

In this query, 'ORDER BY Salary DESC' sorts the salaries in descending order. 'LIMIT 1 OFFSET 1' then selects the second row from the sorted list, which represents the second highest salary.

Both methods have their advantages: The first query is more universally applicable to different SQL implementations, while the second query might be more efficient in large datasets depending on the database's query optimization.

5. **Can you describe a scenario where you demonstrated ability to work under pressure, managing own time to meet tight deadlines.**

When I was the Customer Service Manager at Entain Group, we were given the task of implementing a new loyalty program to boost customer retention. The program's launch date was pre-set to align with a significant marketing campaign and leaving only a tight timeframe for us to prepare everything.

In that high-pressure situation, I started by breaking down the project into smaller, manageable tasks, including team training, program communication, customer queries management, and performance tracking. I assigned a priority level to each task based on its impact on the program's success and set up a detailed project timeline with clear deadlines for each task.

One of the biggest challenges was training the team on the new loyalty program while ensuring regular customer service wasn't disrupted. I managed this by organising short, frequent training sessions during quieter hours and created a comprehensive handbook that the team could refer to at any time.

Simultaneously, I prepared communication scripts to explain the new program to customers succinctly, and planned ahead for potential customer queries, preparing responses for the team to use.

Finally, to ensure we could track the performance of the loyalty program from day one, I worked with our IT team to set up tracking within Power BI. Despite the tight deadlines, we successfully launched the loyalty program on time, which significantly boosted our customer base and retention rates.

This experience taught me the value of detailed project planning, time management, and effective delegation when working under pressure.

6. **Could you tell me about a time when you had to explain a complex concept or procedure to a colleague or client? How did you ensure they understood?**

I can recall a situation during my time as a Customer Service Manager at the Entain Group. We had introduced a new customer loyalty program which used a slightly complex model of points and rewards. My team was required to understand this model thoroughly in order to explain it to our customers effectively.

I arranged a meeting with my team and started by explaining the basic concept of the program, the benefits for the customers, and how it could impact our sales. I used clear and straightforward language and included examples to make sure they understood. I also created a simplified version of the model using diagrams and flowcharts to visually explain the system.

After my explanation, I encouraged questions and discussions. This provided a platform for team members to express any confusion or doubts. I found that this approach not only clarified their understanding but also helped identify potential issues that we were able to address upfront.

To ensure the team fully understood, I created a quick quiz that comprised various scenarios they might face when explaining the loyalty program to customers. Their responses helped me gauge their comprehension and provide further clarification where needed.

Throughout this process, I ensured that all communications were open, engaging, and interactive, so everyone felt comfortable asking questions. This, I believe, is the key to successful knowledge transfer and mutual understanding.

7. Can you recall a situation where you had to make a difficult decision in a short amount of time? What was the decision, and what was the outcome?

I can share an example from when I was working as a Bar Manager at Chai Ki.

On one particularly busy night, we were hosting a large party that had been pre-booked for months. Unfortunately, on the same day, one of our key bartenders called in sick, leaving us understaffed. This was a significant problem because we had to maintain our service quality for the party as well as serve our regular customers.

In such a short notice situation, the options were limited. We could either carry on with the remaining staff, which could lead to decreased service quality, or I could step in and fill the gap despite my managerial responsibilities.

I decided to step in as the bartender for the evening, delegating some of my managerial duties to a senior team member whom I trusted. I made this decision because I knew my bartending skills were proficient and that the senior team member was capable of handling the delegated tasks.

The result was quite positive. We managed to successfully cater to the party, as well as our regular customers. We received compliments for our service that night, and the senior team member appreciated the additional responsibility, which turned out to be a confidence booster for him.

This experience showed me the importance of quick decision-making, adaptability, and trusting your team in crisis situations. It reinforced the idea that sometimes leaders need to step into frontline roles to keep operations running smoothly.

8. **Tell me about a time when you identified a new, unusual or different approach for addressing a problem or task.**

I'd be happy to share an example from my tenure at Entain Group. While I was a Customer Service Manager there, we faced a consistent issue of long customer wait times during peak hours. Our traditional approach was simply to add more staff during those times, but this solution was not sustainable in the long run due to cost constraints.

I decided to take a data-driven approach to this problem. Using SQL, I collected and analyzed data on customer arrival times, duration of service, and number of staff on duty. I combined this data with customer feedback to understand their pain points more accurately.

Upon analysis, I noticed a pattern where specific services took longer than others, causing a backup during peak hours. Armed with this information, I proposed a solution where we would create 'express lanes' for quicker services during peak hours.

The team was initially skeptical about this unusual approach. However, I explained my analysis and how this could potentially reduce wait times without incurring the cost of additional staff. They agreed to run a pilot program.

To our delight, the new system significantly reduced wait times, increased customer satisfaction, and also boosted the morale of the customer service team who felt less pressured. This taught me the value of data analysis in problem-solving and how sometimes, unconventional approaches can lead to great results.

9. Can you share an instance where you went above and beyond to meet a customer's needs or exceed their expectations?

Certainly, during my time as a Customer Service Manager at the Entain Group, we focused on going the extra mile for customers regularly. One instance that stands out involved a long-standing customer who was a part of our loyalty program.

This customer, Mrs. Green, was a senior citizen who came to our shop every week for years. One day, Mrs. Green informed us that due to her deteriorating health condition, she would no longer be able to visit our shop. This was disappointing news, not only because we were losing a loyal customer, but also because we had built a good rapport with Mrs. Green over the years.

After some brainstorming, I decided to coordinate a home delivery service for Mrs. Green, ensuring she could still get her favorite items without the need to travel. Although our company didn't traditionally offer home delivery, I made an exception in this case considering Mrs. Green's loyalty and circumstances.

When we informed Mrs. Green about this arrangement, she was overjoyed and deeply grateful. This not only helped us retain a loyal customer but also spread positive word-of-mouth about our customer service.

This experience taught me the importance of empathy in customer service and that sometimes, thinking outside the box and going the extra mile can make a significant difference to customer loyalty and satisfaction.

10. Tell me about a time when you received challenging feedback from a client. How did you handle it?

During my time at the Entain Group as a Customer Service Manager, we regularly gathered feedback from our customers to improve our service quality.

One time, we received some critical feedback from a long-time client, Mr. Smith, who expressed dissatisfaction with the changes we made in our loyalty program. He believed that the changes reduced the value he was getting and was considering taking his business elsewhere.

Initially, it was quite challenging to receive such negative feedback from a long-time client. But I realized it was an opportunity for us to improve and possibly rectify the situation. I reached out to Mr. Smith, thanking him for his feedback, and arranged a meeting to discuss his concerns in person.

During the meeting, I listened carefully to his concerns and apologized for any inconvenience caused. I then explained the reasons behind the changes in the loyalty program, making sure he understood our intentions were to offer more diverse rewards to our broad customer base.

Nevertheless, I recognized his dissatisfaction and proposed a personalized solution to ensure he still got great value from the loyalty program. The solution involved offering Mr. Smith additional benefits that aligned with his preferences and shopping habits.

Mr. Smith appreciated our prompt and considerate response. He agreed to continue with our revised loyalty program and appreciated the personalized solution we offered. From this experience, I learned the importance of treating challenging feedback as an opportunity to improve and deepen relationships with clients, by demonstrating your commitment to their satisfaction.

11. **Can you describe a time when you were particularly proud of the balance between the quality and efficiency of your work?**

Yes, I'd be happy to share. In my role as a Customer Service Manager at the Entain Group, one of my key responsibilities was improving the efficiency of our daily operations while ensuring high standards of quality.

One incident that stands out involved the restructuring of our customer loyalty program. With an increasing number of customers, it became challenging to maintain the same level of personalized service while ensuring efficiency in the delivery of the program's benefits.

I saw an opportunity to use data analytics to streamline our approach. Using Power BI, I started tracking and measuring performance data related to our loyalty program. We gathered information on customer preferences, purchasing behaviors, response times, and satisfaction levels. Through analysis of this data, I was able to identify patterns and trends that helped us understand where we could make improvements without sacrificing the quality of our service.

We restructured our customer loyalty program based on these insights, which resulted in a more efficient process that maintained a high level of personalized service. By segmenting our customers based on their preferences and shopping habits, we were able to tailor the benefits of the program more effectively, which increased customer satisfaction.

This project not only improved efficiency but also resulted in a boost in customer retention rates, demonstrating the successful balance between quality and efficiency. I was particularly proud of this project because it showcased the power of data-driven decision-making and its impact on improving business operations and customer satisfaction.

12. **Tell me about a time when you had to juggle several tasks at once. How did you organize your time to ensure you achieved results?**

In my role as Bar Manager at Chai Ki, multitasking and time management were crucial to my daily operations. A specific instance I remember is when we were hosting a large event, while still managing our regular operations.

We had a corporate event that was to be held in one of our larger spaces, catering to around 100 guests. Meanwhile, the restaurant was still open to our regular patrons. As the Bar Manager, I was responsible for coordinating beverage services for both the event and regular operations, managing staff, inventory, and ensuring a high level of customer service.

First, I delegated tasks to the team based on their strengths and skills. I assigned a dedicated team for the event and a separate team for the restaurant operations. I also set clear expectations and communicated the priorities and deadlines to ensure everyone was aligned.

Next, I made sure to keep track of inventory and pre-planned any additional supplies needed. This helped to avoid last-minute rushes and ensured smooth service. I also established check-in points throughout the evening to address any concerns or issues immediately.

Simultaneously, I used my time management skills to stay on top of both the event and restaurant operations. This involved regularly circulating between the event and the bar, troubleshooting any issues, and ensuring that our service was up to our usual high standards.

As a result, the event went off smoothly, with positive feedback from the corporate client, and our regular operations didn't face any disruptions. This experience was a testament to effective multitasking, team management, and the importance of clear communication and organization.

13. **Please share an experience when you worked in a team and faced conflict or difficulty. How did you handle the situation?**

I believe teamwork often brings about some challenges alongside its many benefits. There was a situation during my tenure as a Bar Manager at Chai Ki where we had a conflict in the team that required resolution.

We had two team members who had a disagreement over work distribution. One felt that they were being given a heavier workload compared to the other. This disagreement started to affect the atmosphere and productivity of the entire team, and as their manager, I felt it was essential to address it quickly and effectively.

First, I arranged a private meeting with both individuals to listen to their perspectives separately. This gave them a safe environment to express their concerns without feeling judged or interrupted. I made sure to actively listen, empathise, and validate their feelings.

Next, I arranged a meeting with both team members together. I encouraged each to share their point of view while asking the other to listen without interrupting. Once both had aired their concerns, we discussed the division of duties and how we could make it feel more equitable to both. It was essential to emphasise that the goal was to ensure everyone felt treated fairly and that our ultimate goal was to work together harmoniously for the betterment of our services.

To monitor the progress, I established a regular check-in with both of them and the broader team to ensure open communication and address any further issues promptly.

In the end, both team members understood each other's perspectives better and agreed to a more evenly distributed set of responsibilities. This situation helped to foster better communication within the team and reinforced the importance of open dialogue in maintaining a positive and productive work environment.

14. Can you share a time when you helped a team member understand their role in achieving team objectives?

Certainly, there was an occasion during my tenure as a Customer Service Manager at Entain Group that stands out.

One of our team members, who was relatively new, was struggling to understand how their individual tasks contributed to the overall objectives of our customer loyalty programme. The team member was responsible for handling customer queries, providing product information, and driving customer sign-ups for the loyalty programme. However, they viewed their role as independent transactions rather than an integral part of the overall customer retention strategy.

I took the opportunity to have a one-on-one conversation with this team member. I started by explaining the overarching objective of the loyalty programme, which was to enhance customer retention and improve customer lifetime value. I then mapped out how their role tied into this goal.

For instance, their interaction with customers was not just transactional but an opportunity to improve customer relations, build trust, and promote our loyalty program. I highlighted how each sign-up they achieved contributed to our overall customer base and improved customer retention rates.

Furthermore, I used specific data and reports from Power BI to demonstrate the direct impact of their work. Seeing the tangible outcomes and how their efforts influenced our customer retention metrics helped them understand the larger picture.

The team member found this session extremely beneficial. With a clearer understanding of their role within the broader team objectives, their motivation and performance improved noticeably. They started taking more initiatives to sign up customers for the loyalty programme and came up with suggestions to make the process more seamless.

This experience highlighted for me the importance of every team member understanding not just their role, but also how they contribute to the larger objectives of the team and organisation.

15. Can you tell me about a time when you had to manage a relationship with a difficult colleague or client?

Let me share an instance from my time as a Bar Manager at Chai Ki.

In our industry, we often had to liaise with representatives from different beverage companies. There was one particular representative who was known to be quite challenging to deal with. They were often rigid in negotiations and dismissive of our restaurant's needs.

The first few interactions I had with them were difficult. It was a challenge to get them to acknowledge our requirements or be open to any form of negotiation. Rather than get frustrated, I saw this as an opportunity to leverage my relationship management and communication skills.

I decided to take a step back and invest time in understanding their perspective. In one of our meetings, I casually asked about their role and the pressures they were facing. It turned out that they were under significant stress to meet certain targets and felt they had little room for flexibility.

Once I understood this, I changed my approach. I made sure our conversations were more collaborative. I clearly articulated our requirements but also asked about their targets and how we could potentially help them meet these. This mutual exchange created a more understanding and cooperative environment.

Over time, this difficult relationship transformed into one of our most productive ones. We managed to strike several deals that were beneficial for both parties. The representative also appreciated this approach and was more receptive and understanding in our discussions.

This experience taught me the value of patience, understanding, and open communication in managing difficult relationships. It reinforced that taking the time to understand the other party's perspective and objectives can significantly help in finding common ground and fostering positive relationships.

16. **Describe a situation when you had to leverage your relationship skills to drive a project or meet a business objective.**

I recollect my time as a Customer Service Manager at Entain Group.

There, we were implementing a new customer loyalty program, with a goal to expand our customer base and improve retention. However, despite our marketing efforts, the program wasn't getting the expected traction in the initial weeks.

I recognised the need to get our front-line staff - the team members interacting directly with customers - more invested in the program. They had the power to significantly influence customer decisions, but for that, they needed to believe in the program themselves.

To get them onboard, I started by scheduling a series of meetings where I openly discussed the program's objectives, benefits, and the role it played in our larger business goals. I used these meetings as a platform to engage in open dialogue, answering questions, addressing concerns, and even taking feedback on what we could do better.

In addition, I made it a point to personally connect with each team member, understanding their motivators and challenges, and explaining how their individual efforts contributed to the overall success of the program. I also recognised and rewarded those who were making significant efforts to promote the program, further motivating the team.

This relationship-centric approach paid off. We saw increased enthusiasm among team members in promoting the program, which in turn translated to a noticeable uptick in program sign-ups and customer engagement. In fact, we started to track and measure the performance using Power BI to understand the improvement better.

This experience reaffirmed to me that relationship management is not just about managing relationships outside the organization, but also within. By nurturing strong, transparent relationships with the team, we were able to drive better business results.

17. Why do you want to be a Business Analyst?

My fascination with Business Analysis stems from its pivotal role in bridging the gap between IT and business goals. This field allows for strategic problem-solving, a strength I have honed over the years. It gives me the opportunity to leverage my analytical skills, my understanding of data analysis tools like SQL, and my knack for creating impactful data visualisations in tools like Tableau and Power BI.

My previous roles, notably as a Customer Service Manager, have given me a taste of using data to inform decision making, improve processes, and ultimately contribute to a company's growth. For instance, I've successfully used Power BI to track customer loyalty program targets, which significantly enhanced our customer retention rates.

In addition, I'm drawn to the dynamic nature of the role. Business Analysts have the unique position of being involved in various aspects of a project - from initial conception to final implementation. It's this variety and the constant opportunity to learn and grow that excites me about becoming a Business Analyst.

Moreover, having researched about Diligenta and its focus on transforming businesses, I believe that it's an environment where I can make significant contributions while also further honing my skills.

18. What are your long-term career goals, and how does this role align with those goals?

My long-term goal is to become an expert in leveraging data to drive strategic business decisions, essentially evolving into a role such as a Senior Business Analyst or a Data Analyst. I also aspire to lead teams in complex projects, ensuring efficient delivery and contributing towards the organization's strategic goals.

This Graduate Trainee – Business Analysis role at Diligenta aligns perfectly with my goals. It offers a platform to develop competence in Business Analysis and understanding of different delivery lifecycles that Diligenta operates. This role will also allow me to gain a rounded understanding of Diligenta, the wider TCS Group, and its position in the outsourcing market within Financial Services.

The opportunity to engage in diverse tasks, including project management duties, analysing business requirements, reporting on results and performance, and assisting with testing, will help me grow both in breadth and depth of the field. This progression is fundamental to reaching my career objectives.

Moreover, Diligenta's focus on developing effective stakeholder management skills and understanding of the financial services regulated environment further aligns with my career goal of becoming a leader in the field. It will provide me with the foundational knowledge necessary to navigate, contribute and eventually lead in the business analysis landscape.

19. You mentioned that you have experience with Power BI. Can you give an example of a report you created and how it was used?

I have experience using Power BI in my role as a Customer Service Manager at Entain Group.

One significant report I created was a dashboard that tracked the performance of our customer loyalty program. The data set was fairly large, comprising various metrics like the number of customers enrolled, customer retention rate, frequency of purchases, and overall customer satisfaction levels.

I used Power BI to create a comprehensive, interactive dashboard that presented these metrics in an easily digestible format. The visuals included a combination of pie charts, bar graphs, and trend lines. I also implemented drill-down features, allowing users to explore data at more granular levels, such as by region or by the specific loyalty program.

This Power BI report was used by our team and the management to monitor the effectiveness of our loyalty programs. The visualizations helped us quickly identify patterns and trends, spot any potential issues, and measure our progress against KPIs.

For instance, if a particular loyalty program was not performing well in a certain region, we could quickly spot this trend in the dashboard and investigate further. This allowed us to make informed decisions, such as adjusting our strategy or reallocating resources, to improve our customer retention rates and overall customer satisfaction.

The project was a great success and was appreciated for its intuitive design and the actionable insights it provided. It not only made our team more data-driven but also enhanced our ability to make swift, informed decisions.

20. How has your experience as a Customer Service Manager prepared you for a role as a Business Analyst?

My experience as a Customer Service Manager has prepared me for a Business Analyst role in several ways.

Firstly, my role involved a substantial amount of data analysis and interpretation. I utilized Power BI to track and measure the performance of our customer loyalty program targets. This involved creating dashboards, interpreting data, and making informed recommendations based on my findings. These are core skills of a business analyst.

Secondly, as a Customer Service Manager, problem-solving was a daily task. Whether it was dealing with a customer complaint, addressing a team dispute, or optimizing our processes, I learned how to approach problems methodically and creatively. Business analysts often face complex problems and have to come up with efficient solutions - a skill I've honed in my role.

Another crucial aspect was the necessity to understand and improve customer experiences. In the Business Analyst role, understanding end-users (who can be seen as internal customers) and their needs is paramount to create solutions that align with their expectations.

Lastly, project management was a significant part of my role, which often meant juggling multiple tasks, meeting tight deadlines, and coordinating with different teams. In the role of a Business Analyst, this experience will be beneficial in managing various stakeholders, prioritizing tasks, and ensuring that projects are delivered on time and within scope.

Overall, my time as a Customer Service Manager has provided me with a solid foundation in data analysis, problem-solving, project management, and user experience understanding - all of which are critical skills for a Business Analyst.

21. Can you explain your Exploratory Data Analysis Project on World happiest countries analysis?

This project was primarily designed to analyse various factors influencing the happiness index of countries worldwide. It involved a detailed exploration of a large dataset sourced from the World Happiness Report, which incorporates several indicators such as GDP per capita, social support, healthy life expectancy, freedom to make life choices, generosity, and perceptions of corruption.

To begin with, I used SQL and Excel for data cleaning and initial explorations, dealing with any missing or inconsistent data. I also created some derived columns that I thought might be useful for my analysis.

After that, I ran an extensive exploratory data analysis, aiming to find patterns, spot anomalies, and test hypotheses. I mainly focused on understanding the relationship between different variables and how they impact a country's happiness score. For example, I investigated whether there was a significant correlation between GDP per capita and happiness score, which indeed, there was.

I also grouped the countries by regions to see if regional factors played a role in happiness levels. This was an interesting aspect as it highlighted how cultural, societal, and regional aspects could affect the happiness index.

The analysis also involved a comparison of the happiest and unhappiest countries to determine what the most significant contributing factors were in each case.

I presented my findings using various data visualisation techniques, ensuring the results were easy to understand for non-technical team members or stakeholders.

22. Tell me about a time when you had to learn a new tool or technology to complete a task or project.

Learning new tools and technologies has been a crucial part of my career progression, and I am always open to mastering new skills.

One specific instance that stands out is when I was a Customer Service Manager at Entain Group, where I was tasked with tracking and measuring the performance of our customer loyalty program. At that time, we were looking for a more advanced tool that could help us visualize our data more effectively. I discovered that Power BI could provide a robust solution to our requirements.

While I had previously been using Excel for data analysis, Power BI was a completely new tool for me. I recognised that this software had excellent potential to offer a much more interactive and dynamic way of presenting data.

I began by taking online tutorials and studying documentation to familiarize myself with the features and capabilities of Power BI. I then started to implement what I had learned, experimenting with the tool, creating sample dashboards, and testing out different features. It was a challenging yet exciting learning curve. I had to manage my time effectively to learn Power BI while also performing my daily responsibilities.

Once I was comfortable with the tool, I developed a dashboard for our team that tracked key performance indicators related to our customer loyalty program. This dashboard helped us understand our performance better and identify areas where we could improve. My team appreciated the new insights, and it eventually led to an improvement in our customer retention rate.

This experience has strengthened my belief in continuous learning and upskilling. It taught me how mastering a new tool can significantly enhance our efficiency and effectiveness. It also served as a reminder that stepping out of our comfort zone often leads to growth and improvement.

23. What was your most challenging project or task in your previous roles, and how did you handle it?

One of the most challenging projects I faced was during my tenure as a Customer Service Manager at Entain Group. I was given the task to improve our shop's rating standard, which was underperforming at the time due to some operational and customer service issues.

First, I had to understand the problems thoroughly. I conducted an extensive analysis of customer feedback and our operational procedures, discovering a few critical areas for improvement. These included lack of proactive communication to customers, unclear workflow procedures among team members, and missed opportunities in executing our loyalty programs.

The next step was to implement the solutions. I worked on improving our communication with customers, making it more proactive and focused on their needs. I also reviewed and streamlined our workflow procedures, ensuring they were clear, efficient, and effectively communicated to the team.

A key part of this project was to enhance the execution of our loyalty programs to expand our customer base and boost retention. For this, I used Power BI to track and measure our performance. I developed a dashboard that displayed key performance indicators related to the program, which helped us better understand our progress and identify areas needing improvement.

This project was challenging not only because of its complexity and the significant impact it could have on our business, but also because it required careful coordination between different areas of the business and managing change among the team. However, with open communication, effective collaboration, and continuous monitoring of our performance through Power BI, we were able to successfully improve our shop rating standard.

This experience taught me the importance of data-driven decision-making, teamwork, and being proactive in addressing issues. It also highlighted how valuable resilience and adaptability are in navigating complex projects.

24. Can you describe Research Project at UWE where you Collected and analysed Quantitative & Qualitative data for understanding consumer ethical purchase actions. (SPSS)?

The primary aim of the project was to understand the factors influencing consumers' ethical purchase decisions. We focused on both quantitative and qualitative data to get a comprehensive understanding of the topic.

In the first phase, we distributed online surveys to a broad demographic. These questionnaires were designed to capture quantitative data on ethical purchasing habits, including frequency of ethical purchases, types of products purchased, and the influence of brand reputation on these decisions. We used various statistical techniques in SPSS, such as regression analysis and ANOVA, to understand patterns, relationships and differences within the data.

In the second phase, we conducted in-depth interviews with a select group of consumers. This helped us gain qualitative insights into the motivations behind ethical purchases, the perceived value of ethical products, and the influence of societal norms and peer influence on ethical purchasing behaviour.

Analyzing both types of data provided a comprehensive understanding of consumer behaviour in relation to ethical purchasing. The quantitative data helped us identify general trends and patterns, while the qualitative data provided rich insights into the motivations and experiences of individual consumers.

The project was challenging due to the vast amount of data and the need for careful analysis. However, it taught me invaluable lessons about consumer behaviour, ethical decision-making, and how to effectively use tools like SPSS for data analysis. This experience directly translates to the role of a Business Analyst, where understanding data and making data-driven decisions is critical.

25. Can you explain the difference between INNER JOIN, LEFT JOIN, and RIGHT JOIN in SQL, and give an example of a situation where you might use each?

The three types of joins you mentioned, INNER JOIN, LEFT JOIN, and RIGHT JOIN, are SQL commands used to combine rows from two or more tables based on a related column.

1. INNER JOIN: This type of join returns records that have matching values in both tables. For instance, if we have two tables - 'Customers' and 'Orders', and we want to find out all the customers who have made at least one order, we will use an INNER JOIN.

SELECT Customers.CustomerName, Orders.OrderID

FROM Customers

INNER JOIN Orders

ON Customers.CustomerID = Orders.CustomerID;

2. LEFT JOIN (or LEFT OUTER JOIN): This join returns all records from the left table (Customers), and the matched records from the right table (Orders). If there is no match, the result is NULL on the right side.

SELECT Customers.CustomerName, Orders.OrderID

FROM Customers

LEFT JOIN Orders

ON Customers.CustomerID = Orders.CustomerID;

3. RIGHT JOIN (or RIGHT OUTER JOIN): This join returns all records from the right table (Orders), and the matched records from the left table (Customers). If there is no match, the result is NULL on the left side.

SELECT Customers.CustomerName, Orders.OrderID

FROM Customers

RIGHT JOIN Orders

ON Customers.CustomerID = Orders.CustomerID;

These join types were critical during my Exploratory Data Analysis Project on the world's happiest countries. I used INNER JOIN to match data from two tables - one holding the happiness scores and the other containing economic indicators like GDP per capita. LEFT JOIN was used when I wanted to keep all countries in my analysis, even if they didn't have a matching record in the economic indicators table. RIGHT JOIN was less frequently used in my project, but it could be handy in situations where I wanted to ensure all records from a certain table were included in the results, regardless of whether they had a match in the other table.

26. What are different kinds of requirements in a requirements document? Can you explain with examples.

The Business Analysis Body of Knowledge (BABOK) is a comprehensive guide for business analysts which defines the skills, knowledge, and competencies required to effectively perform business analysis tasks. According to the BABOK guide, requirements are classified into four categories:

1. Business Requirements: These are high-level requirements that reflect the strategic goals of the organization. They express the reasons why a project has been initiated, capturing an organizational goal or objective. An example of a business requirement might be: "We need to increase the overall efficiency of the production line to improve our market competitiveness."

2. Stakeholder Requirements: These are the needs and expectations of the stakeholders involved in the project. These requirements are more detailed than business requirements and serve to bridge the gap between business and solution requirements. For instance, a stakeholder requirement might be: "The production manager needs a daily report of all production line stoppages and their causes."

3. Solution Requirements: Solution requirements describe the features, functionalities, and characteristics of a system. They are further divided into two categories:

   - Functional Requirements: These describe the behaviour and operations a system will be able to perform. For example, "The system must automatically send a notification to the production manager whenever there is a stoppage in the production line."

   - Non-Functional Requirements: These describe the environmental conditions or qualities where the system must operate, often related to performance, security, usability, etc. An example of a non-functional requirement is: "The system must respond to user requests within two seconds."

4. Transition Requirements: These describe the conditions that must be fulfilled to transition from the current state to the future state. They depict temporary scenarios or capabilities, like data migration, user training, etc. For example, "Existing production data must be migrated to the new system, and users must be trained on the new system before it goes live."

Each of these requirement types play an integral role in the planning, design, and execution of business strategies and projects. They ensure that everyone involved has a clear understanding of the objectives and constraints of the project, leading to better outcomes and greater project success.

In my role as a Business Analyst Graduate Trainee at Diligenta, I would be working with stakeholders to understand and document these requirements, helping to ensure that the developed solution/system meets the needs of both the business and the users.

Business Analyst Job Search Tips

Finding the right Business Analyst position is not just about scrolling through countless job postings; it requires a strategic and diligent approach. Understanding the job market, recognizing allied roles, utilizing top job portals, and engaging proactively with recruiters are some of the essential steps that can lead you to your ideal job. Here, we will explore these aspects in detail:

1. Understanding Business Analyst Allied Roles:

In your job search, don't limit yourself to only one specific title. The Business Analyst field is broad and includes various related roles that might fit your skills and interests. Consider expanding your search to include the following allied roles:

- Business Systems Analyst

- Data Analyst

- Process Analyst

- Project Analyst

- Test Analyst

- Systems Analyst

- Technology Analyst

- Reporting Analyst

- Functional Analyst

- Operations Analyst

- Project Manager

These roles may offer similar responsibilities and challenges, and your background and knowledge in business analysis may translate well into any of them.

2. Applying for Roles in Familiar Sectors:

Leveraging your previous sector experience can significantly enhance your chances of landing a BA role. Potential employers often favour candidates who already understand the sector's dynamics, customer needs, processes, and challenges. For example, if Emily, who has retail experience, applies for a Business Analyst role in a retail company, she is likely to stand out in the recruiter's eyes. Her familiarity with the sector could give her an edge over other candidates who may lack that industry-specific knowledge.

3. Utilize Top Job Portals:

Rather than randomly searching through numerous job sites, focus on the top 2 job portals for your country, such as LinkedIn or JobServe. These platforms are known for their comprehensive listings and connections to reputable companies. They provide valuable networking opportunities and often offer features to enhance your job search, such as personalized alerts and job recommendations.

4. Building Rapport with Recruiters:

Finding a job is a job in itself, and simply applying online may not be enough. Taking the initiative to call and build rapport with the recruiter after applying can set you apart from other candidates. A personal touch helps to showcase your suitability, enthusiasm, and commitment to the role. It not only increases your chances of being shortlisted but also creates a positive impression before the interview process.

5. Persistence and Patience:

Remember, the job search process may be time-consuming and challenging. Persistence and patience are key. Keep refining your approach, continue networking, and stay focused on your goals. Regularly update your skills and always be prepared for new opportunities.

The journey to finding the right Business Analyst position can be complex, but with a strategic approach, you can navigate it successfully. By exploring allied roles, leveraging top job portals, engaging proactively with recruiters, and maintaining diligence, you will enhance your job search experience. Embrace the process as a learning opportunity and remain committed to finding the position that aligns with your career path and ambitions.

Conclusion

As we close the pages of "Become a Business Analyst: Real Life CASE STUDIES with solutions to help you LEARN FAST and CRACK INTERVIEWS!", I hope that you feel equipped, inspired, and energized to forge your path in the world of business analysis. This comprehensive guide has led you through a multifaceted journey, from understanding the ubiquity of business analysis to exploring case studies across industries and diving into the nitty-gritty of resume preparation and interview strategies.

The road to excelling as a Business Analyst is paved with continuous learning and practical application. The case studies, real-life interviews, tips, and tools provided in this book are just the starting point. Your ability to adapt, innovate, and apply these principles will define your success.

Remember that the landscape of business analysis is dynamic and vast. The case studies in this book, ranging from orchestrating office relocations to enhancing AI operations, are a testament to its diversity and excitement. I urge you to keep questioning, exploring, and applying these insights in your professional endeavours.

Whether you are transitioning into a Business Analyst role, eyeing a promotion, or simply expanding your toolkit, this book has opened the doors to an exciting realm. Your curiosity, perseverance, and the practical wisdom gleaned from these pages set you on the path to mastery in business analysis.

I want to thank you for embarking on this enriching journey with me, and I invite you to stay connected. Whether it's sharing your experiences, seeking advice, or engaging with career coaching services on Fiverr, I'm here to support you. Reach out via email at BACareerStrategy@gmail.com or leave me a review on Amazon.

Here's to your burgeoning success in the world of business analysis. Embrace the adventure and take your newfound skills and confidence into the exciting future that awaits you.

PS: For personalized support, including resume creation or mock interviews, don't hesitate to explore my career coaching services on Fiverr. Link to Fiverr Profile: https://www.fiverr.com/manmeetsingh335

Good luck and take care!

Made in United States
Troutdale, OR
07/01/2024

20925644R00189